MORE THAN ENOUGH

MORE THAN ENOUGH

DIANE ALTOMARE

First Printing, 2024

ISBN-13: 978-1-962984-20-1 print edition
ISBN-13: 978-1-962984-21-8 e-book edition

Waterside Productions
2055 Oxford Ave
Cardiff, CA 92007
www.waterside.com

Book design by Boja.

This material has been written and published for educational purposes to enhance one's knowledge and ability to improve emotional and psychological well-being. The content of the book is the sole expression and opinion of the author.
The information given herein is not intended for the diagnosis of any medical condition, and the techniques presented here are not intended to be a substitute for an individual's prescribed medications or therapies.
Throughout this book, stories and examples of typical client experiences are used to illustrate and help the reader better understand the processes described. These stories are not those of actual persons, but are drawn from the writer's imagination and to be interpreted as composites of many people's experiences.

CONTENTS

Advance Praise for *More Than Enough*

"Eloquently written! A must-read guide for individuals and couples. Through personal anecdotes, insightful exercises, and actionable strategies, you are given tools and skills to combat the negative inner dialogue we all experience. Leave it on your desk and read it often."

—DR. SHAILINDER SODHI
President of Ayush Herbs, Inc.

"I've been fortunate enough to work with Diane Altomare. Diane has always been someone who I could turn to to help me cope with the pressures of being on television everyday... from the constant criticism to those little voices in my head that told me I wasn't smart enough, pretty enough, or funny enough. This groundbreaking book is a step-by-step guide to draw on her wisdom and embrace, once and for all, that you're more than enough."

—LISA BRECKENRIDGE
NBC Correspondent & TV Personality

"*More Than Enough* is a powerful book that will train you to transform the mean, negative, limiting voices in your head into a loving, kind, supportive soundtrack that reminds you of how deserving and wonderful you really are. Commit to following the simple, healing exercises provided, and be amazed and delighted at how great your life will be when you learn to love all of yourself."

—ARIELLE FORD
Author, *The Love Thief*

Dedicated with immense love to you, Dad. You have always been home to me. I miss you so much.

INTRODUCTION

Life is quite a whirlwind of breathtaking
magnificence, immense suffering, and everything in
between. I'm beyond grateful to have both endured it
and had the opportunity to share the wisdom I've
gained from it.

For the past two decades, I have had the distinct
honor and privilege of bearing witness to people's
lives—their   challenges,   trauma,   pain,
breakthroughs, epiphanies, growth, and so much of
what it means to travel this journey of life.

Sometimes life is messy, arduous, painful and may
bring us to our knees. Other times it can be glorious,
joyful, breathtakingly beautiful, and can render us
speechless.

It has been one of the greatest joys of my life to be
an integrative life coach.

During hours upon hours of coaching others, I
have had a close-up lens with which to observe
human behavior, the many different decisions we

make, and the way the psyche accumulates and assimilates our past. It has been nothing short of fascinating.

The truth is that each one of us is merely a culmination of all we have experienced in our lives, up and until we take time to reflect on what is going on within us and make a conscious decision to unravel and unpack our past and acknowledge how it has impacted who we have become. From this newfound clarity, we can decide how it will further determine who we are and what is possible for our lives moving forward.

One of the most glaring and profound observations I have made during countless hours of coaching others is that no matter what walk of life someone comes from, each one of us has, at some point in our life, felt *not enough*; not good enough, smart enough, pretty enough, rich enough, talented enough, courageous enough, influential enough, and the list goes on and on. What I have seen at the heart of so many of my clients' struggles, as well as my own, which I will share throughout this book, is that despite how amazingly brilliant, talented, successful, or courageous we may actually be, there is a part of us that is loudly shouting, often harshly criticizing our every move with sentiments like, "You don't measure up, you don't have what it takes—your business, this project, this book, your dissertation, your parenting, your work, *isn't good enough, you're not good enough.*"

It is the sole reason I chose to write this book.

Regardless of whether you're male, female, rich, poor, young, old, successful, have made it through immense challenges in your life or are still stuck in a huge mess that you're not quite sure how to get out of, each one of us has, at some point in our life, felt like we don't measure up. It is undeniably a part of the human condition.

However, what I've also personally experienced and guided thousands of people to embrace is that it doesn't have to define you or hold you back from living your best life. It can be the pathway into your greatest, most glorious self.

This book is the journey back to that truth. To no longer allow the voice in your head that declares, "*I'm not good enough, smart enough, talented enough, courageous enough, attractive enough, there's something wrong with me, I just don't have what it takes...*" to make you feel bad or to stop you from experiencing and embracing the richness this life has to offer. It will also guide you to embrace your greatness and own your unique nature—to deeply connect and illuminate the part of you that knows who you are, that knows you are here for a divine purpose. So,

3

without wasting another precious moment, let's get right to it!

MORE THAN ENOUGH

THE MEAN, CRITICAL VOICE

*I'm done dancing for the world to try to get love,
attention, and validation. Now it's time to simply
dance.*

You know that little voice? That mean-spirited, self-deprecating voice that can break your heart and stop you dead in your tracks? That little whisper in your head that sometimes proclaims:

- I'm not good enough.
- I'm not smart enough.
- I don't have what it takes.

The voice I'm talking about is the one that has threatened you and at times even succeeded in holding you back, defining you, stopping you from sharing your light, emanating your greatness, and living the life you've dreamed of.

This is the voice and expression of our "not-good-enough" self. Many of us know this voice all too well. But even if you aren't consciously aware of the way that it may be wreaking havoc in your life, you too may discover that you're being negatively impacted by this self-sabotaging, dream-killing part of you.

It's the part of you that sometimes declares:

- Why bother, I'm going to fail anyway.
- I'll never succeed.
- Who do I think I am anyway? I can't launch a successful business, write that book, leave this job that I hate, find a partner who truly loves me, or create a life that's fulfilling.

I came to a point many years ago where I was extremely exhausted by this part of me squelching my voice, casting a negative light on just about everything I wanted to do, and making me feel bad about who I was.

I remember sitting in my car one afternoon, one of those gorgeous, sunny Southern California days, while this dark part of me cast doubt on my first manuscript. As I held it tightly in my hand, ready to send it off to one of my dear friends who was previously in the book publishing business, that judgmental, ugly part of me started an internal war.

All the work I had done, all the time I spent, years and years of writing, editing, and sharing my heart and soul, came down to an hour of internal chaos. All that hard work was reduced to sixty heart-wrenching minutes that would either commence in moving forward with this initial baby step toward having my first book published or result in my dream being pushed into the back seat by the fear that was overtaking me in that moment. All I wanted was his advice and his feedback. But the fear of judgment was so debilitating and paralyzing that instead of getting out of the car, I just sat there staring at the manuscript in my lap.

"Why are you just *sitting* here, Diane? Get out of the car and go mail him the book."

"I can't," my *not-good-enough* self said. "He's going to hate it. He's read the best books out there. And this isn't one of them."

Oh boy, I thought. Here we go. "What do you have to lose?," said the part of me that believed in me.

And without hesitation, my negative self arrived

9

on the scene for yet another gut punch, "Everything. My self-respect. Our precious friendship. My belief in myself and what I have to say. Forget it. It's simply *not good enough*."

Suffice it to say, the dialogue between these two parts of me went on and on, minute after minute, in that blazing sun, as I sat there for an hour wrestling with my thoughts, myself, and my future.

Fortunately, I can say that I got out of the car and sent him the book. My first book, *Clarity*, the very book that I'm talking about went on to be a best-selling book, a #1 new release on Amazon, and was featured on seven TV shows, thirty radios shows, and helped thousands of people heal, reclaim their light, create success in their lives, forgive past hurts, and heal difficult relationships. Can you imagine what I and others would've missed out on, if I let my not-good-enough self win that day?

And yet, unfortunately, many of us can say that our not-good-enough self has won arguments just like this one more often than the *"good-enough, go-for-it, you've-got-this"* self has throughout our lives.

Maybe you too have experienced this internal tug of war and are sick and tired of it after twenty, thirty, forty or even fifty years of this foul-mouthed, obnoxious, dream-killing voice and self-sabotaging, diminishing part of you robbing you of the life you truly want to live.

If this is the case, you are in the right place as I will tell you that I am a master of—a true expert of—the not-good-enough self. I've spent a lifetime working to make peace with this part of me, while truth be told sometimes failing miserably as I will share throughout this book, and other times celebrating triumphantly as it quietly relaxed back into the shadows.

Throughout this remarkable journey, one of my greatest accomplishments has been helping others reclaim their light. During hours upon hours of coaching others, I have witnessed the debilitating ways this not-good-enough, limiting self can keep the greatest, most unique human beings from fulfilling their purpose and creating what they desire in their lives. Sometimes it's mind boggling to witness all the light people possess and how quickly they jump to diminish it and discount it.

So what is this journey of embracing your *more-than-enough, you've-got-this, go-for-it* self all about?

Feeling *finally enough* is the experience of:

- No longer searching for somebody or something to fix that which was never broken.
- Embracing that you are everything you could ever desire and so much more.
- Reclaiming your light and owning the unique gift you are.
- And most importantly, sharing that very uniqueness with the world.

Today, at the age of fifty-two, although it took many decades, I can now say that I finally feel *more than enough*. More than enough to follow my heart's desire and to fulfill my life's purpose. More than enough to no longer allow the part of me that sometimes doesn't *feel* good enough to hold me back or determine my destiny. More than enough to be who I am wholeheartedly.

So how did I get here? To this place of freedom. Not searching. Not seeking. Not fixing. Not sabotaging. Not selling my soul to feel good enough for a fleeting moment in time. That's a long story, but one I feel is worth telling.

In sharing how I got here, I hope you are inspired

to find your way too, should you be seeking this wholeness and peace at this point in your journey.

Feeling *finally enough* means you no longer have to:

- Diminish your worth.
- Fight for affection or attention.
- Let self-doubt squelch your truth.
- Sell your soul for love, attention, or validation.
- Sacrifice your well-being.
- Say yes to everything and everyone.
- Bury your dreams.
- Give up on yourself.

Sounds amazing, doesn't it? Let's dive right in by identifying and connecting with what your *not-good-enough* self says to you every day. By getting to know this part of you intimately, you will be able to stop it before it takes over and sabotages your dreams.

THE MEAN, CRITICAL VOICE

We all know that the way we treat ourselves as well as how we talk to ourselves determines everything. Yet, many of us would declare that we simply can't get that negative internal dialogue to stop the mean, judgmental, ranting and raving.

Let's take a look at what's going on by identifying which one of these sounds more like the voice you hear in your head.

The kind, loving voice: *I believe in you. All is well. Don't worry. You're doing amazing. Keep on. I'm here. Everything will be OK. You've got this! Your best is more than good enough.*

The mean, critical voice: *Are you kidding me? Why did you say that? Get it together. Stop doing that. Why can't you be stronger? Why can't you be more like him or like her? What's wrong with you? You'll never follow through. You just don't have what it takes.*

Not only does the way we talk to ourselves determine how we feel but it can also negatively impact our ability to accomplish what we want in our lives. If you tend to hear the *mean, critical voice* more often than the *kind, loving voice*, know that you are not alone. Many of us have this negative internal dialogue running through our minds. It's truly part of the human condition. Nonetheless, it's important to stop and recognize how truly toxic and detrimental this mean, critical voice is to your self-esteem and your ability to create what you desire in your life.

It's also just as essential to remind yourself that every day is a brand-new opportunity to practice being more kind and loving to yourself than you were the day before. And since everything we experience in our lives is a direct result of what's happening within us, taking the time to be nicer, kinder, and gentler with yourself is a more powerful and transformational shift than anything else could ever be.

Let's look at how you can begin this process of taking better care of the precious being you are with the exercises below.

BITE-SIZE EXERCISE

***

Take a few minutes every day for the next seven days to check in with yourself. Close your eyes, take a slow, deep breath, and ask yourself: "Is my mean, critical voice running my day, or am I encouraging myself with love and kindness?" As you acknowledge what's happening, know that you can practice shifting from the mean, critical voice to the kind, loving voice simply by bringing your attention to it.

Want more? Listen as I guide you through the exercise below on audio. Find the audio at www.dianealtomare.com/precious-child-exercise/

THE PRECIOUS CHILD WITHIN EXERCISE

For this exercise, I suggest that you envision yourself as a small child. It's often easier to be kind to ourselves when we picture how detrimental it is to be mean, harsh, and critical to a young child verses our adult self. We may trick ourselves into thinking that as an adult, we are strong enough to handle the self-abuse. Or we may not even be conscious of how it's truly affecting us. Envisioning yourself as a small child is a powerful way to realize the impact your mean, critical inner voice is having on your self-esteem and your ability to create what you desire. And instead, make the powerful shift to talk to yourself in a more kind, loving, encouraging way.

1. Take a slow, deep breath, close your eyes, and think of yourself as a precious, innocent five-year-old child.
2. Imagine what you looked like. Did you have pigtails, long curly hair, or was your hair spiked on top of your head? What do you envision yourself wearing as a five-

year-old? (Grabbing a picture of yourself at this age can be extremely helpful and is a great way to reconnect to yourself and this vulnerable, impressionable child within you.)

3. Take a deep breath and affirm that today and every day for the next fourteen days, your work is to care for this precious, sweet child with kind and loving thoughts, words, and actions.

4. As you see this child sitting down in front of you, begin this process by writing down a list of what you're going to say to this little girl or little boy within you over the next two weeks. Write down positive thoughts and phrases that will fill you up, lift you up, and encourage you. You may want to use the internal dialogue above in the kind, loving voice as a starting point or a guide.

5. Then simply put this list in your phone and three times per day look at these positive, kind, loving thoughts and begin to say them to yourself as you picture this young, precious, sweet child within you receiving this love, validation, and encouragement.

6. Most importantly, every time you hear the mean, critical voice try to take over, simply pause, look at yourself in the mirror, and see yourself as that precious, innocent five-year-old. As you imagine her (or him) crying or hanging their head because of the mean, hateful thoughts, recommit to being kind, loving, and gentle.

Make a commitment to do this every day by putting it in your calendar right now. This simple exercise can shift how you feel about yourself and, in turn, what you are able to create and experience in your life.

As you become aware of how your not-good-enough self has been limiting you and as you begin using the tools I will share throughout this book, you will start to see a shift in the way you treat yourself and what you're able to experience in your life as a result.

In the next chapter, we will dive into how our not-good-enough self is born. The more intimately connected you become to the reason your not-good-enough self doesn't feel worthy enough, good enough, smart enough, talented enough, or "whatever" *not enough* you continually judge yourself for, the easier it will be to have compassion for yourself and begin to shift how you're talking to yourself, which voice you're listening to, and the way you're treating yourself every day. This can truly be a game changer.

2

THE NOT-GOOD-ENOUGH SELF IS BORN

The messages we get from our relationships and from society often differ immensely from the messages of our soul. Pay close attention to which one you are following.

The love of a mother is crucial. Unfortunately, Helena didn't experience the nurturing, comforting warmth of a mother's love during her childhood.

In our first session, she described her mother as cold, aloof, and preoccupied. "She was always doing something, always busy in the kitchen, tidying up, or engulfed in something on her phone instead of being with me. I honestly don't remember her ever playing with me."

"And although she always attended my school events, I never got the feeling that she was proud of me in the way that I saw other moms doting on their kids. I always felt like I let her down. It was a look on her face. Like I didn't measure up to her expectations. That I wasn't good enough."

Helena's *not-good-enough* self was born when she was very young. From early on, she noticed a difference in the way her mom treated her verses how her friends' moms encouraged and supported their daughters.

As kids often do, Helena internalized her mother's indifference toward her and made it mean that she must not be good enough. In an attempt to get love, she started to do things to try to get her mom's attention. She studied extra hard to get straight As in school, she always stayed at practice longer than the other kids to make sure she didn't get less than first place, she kept her room extremely neat, and she held herself to extremely high standards, all to get her mom to pay attention to her, to be proud of her.

She did everything she could in hopes of garnering just a little of the love and attention she craved. But that love never came.

In her adult life, Helena became a family defense attorney to fight for children's rights. She dedicated her life to being the voice for kids who didn't get the love they needed. In that sense, her *not-good-enough self* became a powerful force driving her to contribute her gift to neglected children. However, in her own life, sadly, the void she felt from living a lifetime without a mother's love was inescapable.

The gifts that can arise from not feeling good enough can drive us to do amazing things in the world, making a unique contribution to others. However, unfortunately, no matter how much we do or what we create, these achievements alone can never fully fill the void or erase the pain of the trauma we experienced that caused our not-good-enough self to be born in the first place.

The good news? With focused, intentional, dedicated attention and love, we can make peace with our not-good-enough self. We can stop allowing this part of us to determine the choices we make and impacting our life in a negative way.

HELENA'S JOURNEY TO LOVE

I started Helena's session by asking her to connect with the little girl within her, the little girl who felt overlooked by her mother.

I invited Helena to close her eyes and see that little girl sitting in front of her. "What does she look like and how old is she?" I asked. Helena told me that she looked about seven years old and was so adorable. But the little girl was looking down and appeared to be sad.

"Ask her to tell you what it felt like to not get the love and attention she needed from her mom," I said.

Helena looked into the eyes of that little girl and listened. This is what she heard and what she shared with me, as tears streamed down her face.

I don't know what I ever did to make her hate me so much. My mom hated me. I could feel it. I have never said that out loud until now. But she did. She never hugged me. She never played with me. I tried everything to get her to love me. Now that I think about it, I'm still trying to get love and approval from her to this day.

I invited Helena to stay connected to the little girl's pain, to feel the neglect she felt. I assured her it would help set her free, that this was the path to healing the pain she had been holding onto for over three decades. By honoring what that little girl experienced and allowing her to feel heard, validated, and loved, Helena would ultimately be the one to give herself and the little girl within her the love and attention her mother never did.

YOUR WOUNDED SELF

As you read Helena's story, you may resonate with some of it, or you may not. You may have had a great childhood. Or maybe like Helena, you felt love from one of your parents but not the other. Maybe your parents were busy working and a sibling raised you or had a significant impact on your self-esteem.

Similar to Helena, your not-good-enough self was born through a series of different events in your life. Maybe as a child, somebody said something shameful or hurtful to you, and without consciously realizing it you made it mean something about you. It's highly possible that you are still carrying this negative belief and limitation with you to this very day.

Maybe as a kid, your dad dismissed your needs. You made it mean that you are not worthy of attention. Now, as an adult, you continue this neglect by ignoring what you need and putting other people first.

Or maybe at some point in your life, someone snapped at you when you spoke up and shared your views. The embarrassment you felt at that moment has stayed with you ever since. You made it mean that it's not safe to express yourself. And as a result, throughout your life, you hold onto your ideas instead of sharing them.

Or your sister continually criticized you, telling you how stupid you were. You internalized this as, "I will never measure up." As a result, you shy away from trying new things.

Identifying the messages you received as a child is crucial to understanding why you are the way you are. It will give you insight into how your 'not-good-enough' self has developed over the years and will help you understand how you have become who you are today. In addition, it will direct you toward what you need to embrace or let go of, so ultimately you are no longer directed by this wounded part of you. Instead of feeling less than, you will feel amazing about who you are.

The following exercise will help you to determine the negative messaging you internalized throughout your life. It may have been sometime during your childhood, playing in your neighborhood, trying to get attention at home, or fitting in to a clique at school. Or it could have occurred later in life.

26

As you spend time writing down the negative messages you heard and internalized, you will gain insight into how your not-good-enough self has developed over the years. But more importantly, it will intimately connect you to the voice of this part of you so that when you hear the expression of your not-good-enough self echoing repeatedly in your mind, you will know exactly what is happening and what to do. You will recognize that you are in a moment of choice. You can either unconsciously let it direct your life without realizing how much damage this part of you is doing to your self-esteem, or you can choose to spend time honoring the pain of this part of you by recognizing what's happening and having compassion for yourself instead. This is the key to freedom. Let's look at how you can begin this process of taking better care of the precious being you are with the following exercise.

EXERCISE

Find a quiet place to do this visualization. Close your eyes, and as you take a slow, deep breath, notice the rise and fall of your chest and your abdomen. Take a few more slow, deep breaths, and then start with the first category. Write down what arises in your journal.

CATEGORY ONE: NEGATIVE MESSAGING

Take a few minutes to read this list and identify which negative messages you heard and internalized. Then, next to each message, write down who you heard that from. Either who said that to you directly or who gave you that feeling because of the way they treated you. (Dad, mom, sister, brother, a coach, a teacher, a friend, a spouse.)

Negative messages:

You will never measure up.
You're not smart enough.
You're not important enough.
You never follow through.
Your ideas don't matter.
You never stick to any one thing.

You'll never amount to anything.
You're stupid.
You're lazy.
You're selfish.

A category one journal entry from one of my clients:

You never think about anyone else. You're selfish. (A feeling I got from my mom.)

CATEGORY TWO: WHAT YOU MADE IT MEAN ABOUT YOU.

Now looking at the negative message you wrote down in category one, identify what you made it mean about you. How did that statement make you feel about yourself, your worth, or your ability to accomplish what you desire? Write down what arises in your journal.

A journal entry from one of my clients:

When my mom called me selfish, I made it mean that I am not kind or generous enough.

CATEGORY THREE: HOW IT LIMITS YOU IN YOUR LIFE.

Now, expanding on what you made it mean about you, reread what you wrote in category two, and identify how feeling this way about yourself has limited you in your life. Write down what arises in your journal.

A journal entry from one of my clients:

Judging myself as not kind enough or generous enough has driven me to overcompensate and give too much. I also feel guilty when I try to set boundaries and say no. It often keeps me from taking care of my needs, and I tend to put others' needs before my own. I am always last on the list.

Another example from one of my clients:

1. **Category One:** You will never amount to anything. (My dad said this.)
2. **Category Two:** I made it mean that I'm not disciplined enough or smart enough to be as successful as he was.
3. **Category Three:** Continually criticizing myself and judging myself as not disciplined or smart enough causes me to have self-doubt. I tend to start things and

never finish them because the self-doubt is so overpowering that I eventually just give up. It has affected my confidence and kept me from achieving what I want in my life.

You may be starting to see and understand, like putting pieces of a puzzle together, how your not-good-enough self has become solidified and etched deeply into your psyche.

Your work over the next seven days is to notice when you hear these negative messages pop into your consciousness and remember there is a reason you don't feel good enough. Then, do the exercise you just completed again to identify how it is limiting you.

It may take some time to go through this exercise, writing down each negative message you internalized, and then diving deeper into what you made it mean about you as well as how it's still limiting you in your life.

Take your time with this. You may want to work with one or two negative messages now and then continue to work on this exercise later. It is a great one to earmark and revisit when you feel the negative voice in your head running rampant, taking over, or controlling your day.

THE NOT-GOOD-ENOUGH CYCLE

Once our not-good-enough self is born, it becomes more developed year after year by the ways in which its truth is validated and reaffirmed.

You don't feel *good enough* because your dad didn't give you affection, and what happens when your first boyfriend breaks up with you? The not-good-enough self becomes a bit more solidified. Then in college you don't get into the sorority you want and again, you hear the voice in your head say, "*It's because you're not as pretty or as funny as your best friend who got in.*" After college, you get passed up for the promotion you wanted, and which part of you rears its head? You guessed it. Your *not-good-enough* self. This part of you that doesn't feel good enough starts to take over, thinking harsh, critical, discouraging thoughts, making you feel horrible about yourself.

Year after year and so-called failure after failure, you begin to affirm for yourself that you truly aren't good enough, and the voice in your head gets louder and louder, giving you this detrimental message more often.

Before you are consciously aware of it, you identify more with the part of you that doesn't feel good enough than you do with the part of you that is powerful, wise, and knows you can accomplish your deepest desires.

The story continues until you do something about it. Until you begin to change what you are saying to yourself. Until you believe that the part of you that doesn't feel good enough is just a small part of you and not who you are in totality. Until you connect with the more powerful, life affirming, amazing part of you that feels *more than enough*, the part of you that is powerful, wise, and knows you can accomplish everything you desire.

BITE-SIZE EXERCISE

***

Over the next seven days, notice when a negative message such as, "I'm not worthy, I'm not good enough, I'm not smart enough," pops into your mind. Simply observe it without judging it. Remind yourself that there is a reason that you feel that way, and as you work through the exercises in this book, you will gain insight into not only the reason, you feel not good enough, inadequate, and so on, but you will also learn tools to transcend that limiting belief so that it no longer gets in the way of you living your best life.

You have the power to awaken your *more-than-enough* self and live wholeheartedly through this part of you. In the next chapter, we will dive deeply into exactly how to do this—how to stay connected to the part of you that knows you are brilliant enough, talented enough, courageous enough, and powerful enough to fulfill your life's purpose.

3

BELIEVE IN YOURSELF

*You are brilliant enough, talented enough,
attractive enough, courageous enough, and powerful
enough to fulfill your highest purpose and live your
best life.*

What if you knew you were unique beyond measure? Talented enough to fulfill your life's purpose? More powerful than you ever imagined yourself to be? That with focus, energy, and dedication, you could create your heart's desire? What if you knew without any doubt that you could achieve your biggest dreams?

What if you were told all of this from the moment you were born and wholeheartedly felt this throughout your childhood? What if life validated this truth year after year?

Just imagine what your life might be like today.

Would you have developed a part of you that *doesn't feel good enough*? Or would you know from the depth of your being that you are *more than enough*?

What I know to be true after coaching people for twenty years is that many of us diminish how brilliant, powerful, courageous, and talented we truly are. Little by little, year after year, life has a way of diminishing our confidence and the belief we have in ourselves.

However, with the proper nurturing, love, and care you can reconnect to the knowing that lives within the depths of your soul. The knowing that you are more than enough, brilliant enough, talented enough, and powerful enough to fulfill your life's purpose and live your best life.

That regardless of what you experienced during your childhood, what setbacks or failures you have had, what is happening right now in your life, you can create a different path forward.

Many people have come from incredibly challenging upbringings and have created amazing things in their lives despite their circumstances.

I am one of them. As I share in my first book, *Clarity*, growing up in an alcoholic family was heartbreaking, tumultuous, and an emotional roller coaster. My *not-good-enough* self was born from the desperation of wanting to stop the drinking and somehow control the dysfunctional behavior. I internalized so much of the pain and because I couldn't get the drinking to stop—I unconsciously made it mean that I wasn't good enough, I wasn't lovable enough, there was something wrong with me.

However, there is a silver lining, a huge gift. Because of the great pain in *not* feeling good enough, this part of me drove me to seek answers. My *not-good-enough self* drove me to the path of striving to improve, to evolve, and to find peace with who I am regardless of the negative internal dialogue that may be echoing in my mind, regardless of what's happening in my life, regardless of what I experienced during my childhood.

Ultimately, the pain led me directly to the most extraordinary journey back to my most powerful and authentic self, as well as spending the past twenty years helping others heal and find peace with all of who they are. Despite all that I experienced, I have made peace with my not-good-enough self and have created a life that is fulfilling, joyful, and inspiring.

When we do the work to heal our childhood wounds and reconnect with the part of us that is powerful, wise, and believes in us wholeheartedly, the possibilities for our lives are infinite. If I can do it, you can do it too. You too can heal from whatever trauma you may have experienced. You too can create more than life has conditioned you to believe is possible. You too can rise above the negative messages you unconsciously internalized and create a life you love, a life that is inspiring and fulfilling.

I sometimes have clients say they feel like their life is over, like they are too old, or have made too many mistakes to change anything now. Although you may feel that way at times, it's simply not true. It is never too late.

Every day is a brand-new opportunity to create your life the way you want it to be. To step into your greatness. To own your uniqueness. To love yourself wholeheartedly. With the actions you take. With the thoughts you connect with. With the validation and love you give yourself.

As Debbie Ford shares in her book *Your Holiness,* "There is only one antidote to the internal war that so many of us wage against ourselves before we even get out of bed in the morning, and that antidote is love. No, it's not just love; it's self-love. It includes making the decision to stop putting self-love off to some future date when we've finally become worthy. It's loving ourselves right where we are. For each of us, I believe it takes a shift in perception where we truly understand that there is no more time. It's not going to happen next week or next month or next year. We cannot wait for things to get better, because they won't get better while we're still beating ourselves up emotionally and psychologically and continuing to wage war against ourselves."[1]

You have the choice to learn a new way to care for yourself, a new way to communicate with yourself. You can talk to yourself with love, encouragement, and kindness. You can surround yourself with people who are positive, who believe in you, and who support your greatness and the way you want to live your life. You can align your life with your soul's passion and purpose.

Right now, it is your moment to reclaim this. To affirm that making these choices is your birthright. That changing your life is within your power. And that as you begin to make these inspiring, empowering choices for yourself one moment, one day, and one step at a time, you will create a life that is fulfilling and inspiring to you.

Today, make this commitment to yourself, a commitment to begin anew. And I will guide you step-by-step through exactly how to create your best life despite your upbringing, despite societal conditioning, and despite how you may feel about yourself right now.

Begin with the exercise below that will give you a new way to talk to yourself with love, every day, from this point forward.

Want more? Listen, as I guide you through the "Talk to Yourself with Love" exercise on audio. Find the "Talk to Yourself with Love" audio at www.dianealtomare.com/believe-in-yourself/

EXERCISE

TALK TO YOURSELF WITH LOVE

Find a time every day for the next fourteen days to dedicate seven minutes to the following exercise. Then notice how effortless it is to create your best life when you are all filled up with love and encouragement.

1. Take a deep breath, and as you close your eyes, turn your focus and awareness inside. Affirm for yourself that although there are a lot of challenging experiences in life, you do have control over how you talk to yourself and care for yourself.

Acknowledge that this alone can shift everything.

2. Imagine what you could create in your life and how you would feel about yourself if you woke up every day and said, "*I love you. You're brilliant. You're talented. I'm so proud of you. Your best is good enough. I believe in you. You've got this. Let's create our life the way we want it to be.*" Today is the day to begin this practice. To begin talking to yourself with this truth and love.

3. Take a slow, deep breath and focus your attention on your breath. Notice the rise and the fall of your chest and abdomen with each inhale and each exhale.

4. Breathe into your heart, and allow yourself to connect with all the love you have in your heart. All the love you give to others today is the day to give it to yourself.

5. Put your hand on your heart and breathe this into every cell of your being, allowing it to fill you up with light, love, joy, peace, gratitude, and anything else you may feel during this process.

6. Say to yourself, "*I love you. You're brilliant. You're talented. I'm so proud of you. Your best is good enough. I believe in you. You've got this.*

Let's create our life the way we want it to be."

7. And again, take a deep breath and say to yourself, *"I love you. You're brilliant. You're talented. I'm so proud of you. Your best is good enough. I believe in you. You've got this. Let's create our life the way we want it to be."* Feel it even more deeply this time.

8. And one more time, breathe into your heart, and as you connect with all the love you have in your heart, say to yourself, *"I love you. You're brilliant. You're talented. I'm so proud of you. Your best is more than good enough. I believe in you. You've got this. Let's create our life the way we want it to be."*

9. Before you complete this exercise, make an internal commitment that you will be gentle, kind, and loving to yourself as you continually practice talking to yourself with love and kindness each day, from this point forward.

Your work is to do this every day for the next fourteen days. Fill yourself up with the love that you desire, that you deserve, that you need. And from this place, you will create your best life. Make a commitment to do this by putting it in your calendar now.

I hope you are starting to feel the power of being connected to the part of you that feels *more than enough*. The part of you that is rooting you on, that believes in you, and that knows you can accomplish everything you desire. The part of you that won't allow fear to stop you from fulfilling your purpose or living your best life.

Maybe you are starting to feel a bit of hope, some joy, and the possibilities of what your life could be like by awakening this positivity, this internal ray of sunshine. However, at the same time, you may also feel that staying connected to the part of you that feels *more than enough* is not always easy. I am so with you. Know that you are not alone. This is true for many of us. I have moments when I need to talk myself through the fear or self-doubt I'm feeling, especially when I'm trying something new. *I can't do this, I feel inadequate, I don't have the strength, I don't have what it takes,* are a few of the sentiments I hear berating me in my mind.

While this voice may continue to express its disapproval or downright panic with the direction you are going or what you are doing in your life, know that the more you affirm the presence of the part of you that knows you are enough, the more you speak to yourself with love, the more conscious you are of what's going on within you, the easier it will be to honor your not-good-enough self, listen to the wisdom that arises, and shift back into action, living wholeheartedly from the part of you that feels *more than enough* and believes you can accomplish whatever you desire.

Let's look at how seamless it can be to switch from the part of us that doesn't feel good enough and is attempting to squelch our dreams into connection with the part of us that feels smart enough, powerful enough, and courageous enough to live our best life and fulfill our biggest dreams.

STUCK NO MORE

Let's say you are feeling stuck. You feel like *you* aren't smart enough, influential enough, attractive enough, or talented enough to have or create what you want in your life. Or that something you're specifically doing like starting a new business, writing a book, finding a job that is more aligned with who you are, or even allowing yourself to begin dreaming and envisioning something more for your life isn't possible for you because of the part of you that keeps telling you, *you don't have what it takes, you're simply not good enough.*

Instead of fighting it, be with it. Get present to it. Don't resist it. Just let it be there.

You don't feel good enough at this moment. That's OK. But don't let it take over or change what is possible for you. Simply honor that this is the way you feel right now. Let it be part of your experience. Not the total experience. Just a part of it.

Then begin to observe what is happening within you as you experience what it feels like to feel not good enough. Don't fight it. Let it be there. Allow it to move through you.

I used this very method to process through my feelings as my *not-good-enough self* showed up and tried to steal the show and diminish my confidence when I was writing this book. Here is how I worked through it.

EXERCISE: LET IT BE.

Step One: Observe How You Feel

I don't feel good enough right now. I don't feel like I have what it takes. OK. Be with it. Simply observe how you are feeling without having to do anything about it. Notice where you feel this in your body. Does it feel like a knot in your stomach, intensity in your mind, or an overall feeling of insecurity? Don't make yourself "wrong" for feeling the way you do.

Step Two: Give It a Voice

Write out the *voice of your not-good-enough self.* Listen to what this part of you is saying to you. Write out the fear, the self-doubt, the insecurity you feel about your book, your business, an upcoming event, or a project that you don't feel is good enough. Write it out in what-if statements.

Here are the what-if statements I wrote when I started to doubt this book, what I was writing, and whether it would be powerful enough to help people in the way I intended:

- *What if this book isn't good enough?*
- *What if no one gets what I'm trying to say?*
- *What if it's written in a way that doesn't make sense or doesn't apply to people?*
- *What if it's not brilliant enough?*

Step Three: Write Out What-If Statements

Get present to your what-if statements. Read them aloud a few times and then ask yourself, "OK. What if all that happens?"

Right now, simply be with that. Yes, all of this is possible. Simply let yourself be with the possibility that some of that may happen.

As you sit with the possibility of what you are worrying about, wisdom may arise.

Here is the wisdom that came to me when I sat with the feeling of this book not being good enough:

- I can't control whether someone or anyone will resonate with what I'm saying. But there are many things I can control. And all the success I have created in my life has come from focusing on what I can control.
- I can control the actions I take.
- I can control the energy I put into this book.
- I can control the dedication I give it.
- I can trust that coaching people for twenty years has given me a level of expertise that will translate into powerful words and wisdom that has the power to change lives.
- I can remind myself that I have already

helped thousands of people transform their lives with my first, best-selling, award-winning book, Clarity.

- I can reconnect to the truth that I have also helped thousands of people transform their lives with the coaching, guidance, and wisdom I've given in individual sessions.
- I can embrace all of that.
- I can be open to the possibility of this book being *more than enough*, and I can also be at peace with the possibility that it won't be *good enough*. Both are a possibility. And the only thing I can control is the actions I take and the energy I give it. The rest is out of my control.
- I am at peace with all of this as it is. I can now let go and continue writing.

Being with *what is* creates freedom. By allowing our not-good-enough self to express its fear, insecurity, or self-doubt, by listening to and getting present to what we can control, we can navigate our way to finding peace with what is, what we are feeling, and what is possible.

It gives you, like I shared with my what-if statements about this book, a working dialogue to process through what is going on within you and allows you to get to the truth of who you are and what's possible. It liberates you and frees you from the grips of the part of you that doesn't feel *enough*.

You can then move forward from a place of possibility by focusing on taking actions that are within your control. It releases you from the stronghold of the part of you that doesn't feel enough and catapults you back into action and in alignment with the part of you which feels *more than enough*, that is connected to all the possibilities that are present.

Take a few minutes right now to deepen what you have worked on in this chapter by doing the following bite-size exercise.

BITE-SIZE EXERCISE

***

Diminishing ourselves is something many of us unconsciously do. Over the next seven days, notice when you are diminishing your talent, intelligence, courage, or any other quality you need to create your best life. Then take out your journal and write out these diminishing thoughts. Remind yourself that with the proper nurturing, love, and care you can reconnect to the knowing that lives within the depths of your soul. The knowing that you are more than enough, brilliant enough, talented enough, and powerful enough to fulfill your life's purpose. Then spend time each day acknowledging a time or two in your life when you have exhibited that you are more than enough, brilliant enough, talented enough, or courageous enough.

In the next chapter, we are going to dive into how everything we've looked at so far will translate into you having more of what you want in your life. You will continue to solidify your connection with your more-than-enough self and will begin to see what's truly possible for you and how amazing it feels to create your life from this powerful, inspiring energy.

4

YOUR MORE-THAN-ENOUGH, GO-FOR-IT SELF

When we are born, we feel more than enough. We arrive ready to brazenly take on the world, feeling worthy of everything life has to offer.

This chapter is about creating what you desire by reconnecting wholeheartedly with this truth, with this knowing that lives in the depths of your soul. By bringing the energy of your *more-than-enough, you've-got-this, go-for-it* self into everything you do, you will have access to the courage, resilience, and power necessary to fulfill your biggest dreams.

I know the part of you that *doesn't feel good enough* may have just done an internal backflip, awakening a few butterflies in the pit of your stomach. Don't fret. As you continually do the work to reconnect with your *more-than-enough* self, you will be amazed at how easy and effortless it will eventually feel to continually catapult yourself into action, creating more of what you desire in your life. You will feel empowered. You will feel free. You will no longer be at the whim and mercy of the critical, judgmental ranting and raving of your not-good-enough self.

By getting good at both embracing your *more-than-enough* self as well as honoring the wisdom of the part of you that *doesn't* feel *good enough*, the sky's the limit.

YOUR BIG DREAM

So, what is your big dream? What is it that you want to create? What inspires you?

Do you dream of starting a new business? Writing a book? Landing a job that is inspiring and fulfilling? Creating a work of art? Having a loving relationship? Sharing your brilliance in some profound way? Expressing yourself wholeheartedly?

What have you dreamed of doing that your not-good-enough self has diminished, discounted, or otherwise discouraged you from starting? Maybe you've already started taking steps to fulfill your dreams, but you can't seem to create momentum and achieve what you desire because the mean, critical, judgmental nature of your not-good-enough self keeps telling you:

- This isn't going to work.
- Maybe I really don't know what I'm talking about.
- What I'm doing isn't that unique.
- I always start things and then give up.
- What do I have to say that somebody else hasn't already said?
- I'm not talented enough.
- I'm not disciplined enough to stay consistent.
- I just don't have what it takes.

Many of us have heard a dialogue like this, stopping us from moving forward on an idea. Many of us have had the experience of not feeling good enough and abandoning something we started. Many people have a closet full of incompletions simply because this voice in their head keeps diminishing the value of their idea, criticizing their work, judging themselves as inadequate or not courageous enough, and keeps them from completing what they started.

Instead of listening to this critical, judgmental,

diminishing voice and allowing it to run the show and determine what is possible for you, you will recognize when it starts to bully you and make you feel bad about yourself. You will no longer allow it to run wild and become the director of your life. You will know that it is just a part of you. It is simply a part of your experience. It's not who you are in totality.

At times, however, this may be hard to do. You may identify so strongly with the part of you that doesn't feel good enough that it *does* feel like it defines you. Almost as if it is *who* you are. But it is not.

Right now, repeat this to yourself seven times as you breathe it into every cell of your being.

"The part of me that doesn't feel good enough is simply a part of my experience. It is not who I am."

Take a moment to affirm this for yourself. Feel what it feels like to truly grasp that this part of you is not who you are in totality. Acknowledge how freeing this feels. Acknowledge how much more will be possible in your life when you make a commitment to no longer follow the urgings of the part of you that doesn't feel good enough, to no longer allow this part of you to dictate what actions you take, to no longer allow the fear, the anxiety, or the self-doubt to stop you from creating what you want in your life.

Before you continue, take a few minutes right now to post this truth somewhere you can see it every day: *"The part of me that doesn't feel good enough is simply a part of my experience. It is not who I am."* Put a timer in your phone or a Post-it Note on your computer as a reminder.

At any point in the day when you hear this voice ranting and raving, your work is simply to honor how your not-good-enough self feels, gain the wisdom of it, and then reconnect to what your *more-than-enough* self tells you is possible for you and your life.

As you get more intimately connected with what the voice of your not-good-enough self sounds like and get used to this part of you throwing a fit, like a toddler having a tantrum, you will be able to recognize much more quickly what is happening before it threatens to stop you from moving forward.

This was the focus of one of my new client's very first sessions.

JULIA'S LACK OF MOMENTUM

Julia, a thirty-seven-year-old dietitian, started working with me because she simply could not get her business off the ground. No matter how hard she worked, no matter what she tried, she couldn't sustain any momentum and create the successful business she had dreamed of. Even though she was making a difference in her client's lives, her business growth was stunted.

From the moment we talked, it was clear what was limiting Julia. Like so many of us, the reason she couldn't create what she wanted was hidden in the depths of her childhood.

Julia's mom ran the show in their house. She described her as overbearing and intense. She told me she yelled a lot.

"She was strict and controlling, and my dad never got a word in," Julia said. "Nor did we as kids. Sometimes I would try to tell her what I was thinking, but she left no room for children's opinions or needs. Everything was decided on by her. Most of the time I felt like my feelings and what I thought about things were irrelevant and insignificant to her."

Julia's inability to be heard when she was a child

was one of the things that was limiting the growth of her new business. Her confidence was never fully developed as her voice was squelched from an early age. Her mom literally and figuratively drowned it out.

As a result, she always second-guessed herself and diminished how talented she truly was.

I invited Julia to connect to the little girl within her, the little girl who felt like her feelings and thoughts were insignificant in her mom's eyes. I guided Julia to close her eyes and see that little girl sitting in front of her.

"What does she look like, and how old is she?" I asked. Julia told me that she looked seven years old, and her head was hanging—she looked defeated and lost.

"Ask her to tell you how it felt when her mom quieted her," I said.

Julia looked into the eyes of that little girl and listened. This is what she heard and what she shared with me.

Oh gosh. Wow! I haven't thought about this for a long time. I remember being mad as a little girl. I can see that in her eyes right now. I would often cross my arms, pout, and throw a fit. But no matter what I did, no one ever heard me. My mom was in

the room. My dad was even there. But no one gave
my outbursts much attention at all. After a while,
I gave up the pouting, the throwing tantrums, I just
acquiesced to my reality: what I thought and felt
simply didn't matter.

I invited Julia to stay connected to the little girl's pain, to feel how mad that little girl was, to see how shut down she had become. I assured her that it would give her both the energy and the insight she needed to give that little girl her voice back. By honoring what that little girl experienced, by allowing herself to see how truly detrimental it was to her self-worth and confidence, Julia would ultimately be able to give herself permission to say what she needed to say, to be heard, and to know her true value, possibly for the first time.

In addition to the inner work we did in her session, I gave Julia an assignment to be conscious of the moments that she began to second-guess herself. To take time to identify the voice and expression of the part of her that didn't feel significant, that didn't feel like she was worthy enough for others to listen to her thoughts or her opinion.

Throughout our sessions, Julia began to listen to herself, validate her feelings and express herself, give that little girl her voice back, and as a result, she felt more confident in every area of her life. Her conversations with people became more constructive, and she started to own the impact she had in transforming people's lives. Her business organically grew, and she felt on top of the world both personally and professionally.

EXERCISE

YOUR TURN: IDENTIFY THE VOICE OF YOUR NOT-GOOD-ENOUGH SELF

In this exercise, you will have the opportunity to explore the voice of your not-good-enough self more deeply. By identifying what this voice specifically sounds like, you will be able to head it off at the pass and quickly reconnect to the part of you that believes in you. We will refer to this voice like we did in chapter 1, as the mean, critical voice of our not-good-enough self. Find a quiet place to do this visualization and begin.

1. Close your eyes, and take a slow, deep breath and follow that breath inside noticing the rise and fall of your chest and your abdomen. Take a few slow, deep breaths.

2. Identify an area of your life that you don't

feel good about. Maybe it's your career, your home life, your relationship, your health, and so on.

3. Take a deep breath, and connect with how you currently feel about this part of your life. Do you feel frustrated, inadequate, powerless, sad, unfulfilled? Just breathe into whatever you are feeling and allow yourself to feel what you do without judging yourself or making yourself wrong.

4. Simply notice the rise and the fall of your chest and abdomen, with each inhale and each exhale, as you honor how you are feeling.

5. On your next breath, breathe into your heart and allow yourself to connect with what you want to create more of in this part of your life. Do you want to experience more success, more abundance, more peace, and harmony, feel more alive, feel more fulfilled or inspired? Envision what you most desire in this part of your life. Imagine you can see it as if it has already happened. Envision it in detail. And as you do, jot down some notes about

what it feels like to have accomplished what you desire.

6. Put your hand on your heart and breathe this into every cell of your being, allowing it to fill you up with energy, possibility, joy, peace, fulfillment, inspiration, creativity, resilience, and anything else that may be arising for you.

7. Knowing that you can reconnect to this vision and how it feels at any time, take a deep breath, and allow yourself to connect with the part of you that tells you that you can't create this, or that you can't make this happen. The part of you that diminishes your value, harshly criticizes you, judges you as inadequate, or says you aren't smart enough or courageous enough. The part of you that doesn't feel *enough*.

8. As you take a deep breath, listen to this voice of your not-good-enough self. What do you hear in your mind when you think about starting to work on your book, diving into your business, creating your work of art, expressing yourself wholeheartedly? Does this part of you say, *"This isn't going to work, maybe I really don't know what I'm talking about. What I'm doing*

isn't that unique. I always start things and then give up. What do I have to say that somebody else hasn't already said? Someone else has already done this. I'm not disciplined enough to stay consistent. I just don't have what it takes," or something else?

9. Take a few moments to jot down a few words that describe the voice of your *not-good-enough self* in your journal.

10. As you take another deep breath, honor that there is a reason this part of you feels this way. At some point in your life, something happened to make you feel this way, and you internalized this message. Affirm for yourself that you don't have to allow it to control your life from this point forward. And, although this part of you has kept you stuck or held you back at various times in your life, this part of you also holds wisdom.

11. What is the gift or wisdom of your not-good-enough self? For example, maybe *not feeling good enough* is communicating that you need to be more prepared or work on something more diligently for it to be complete or competitive. Maybe you need to do more research or get support,

guidance, or coaching on something you aren't skilled at. Or perhaps feeling not good enough has become a default way of being for you. And there isn't anything you need to change, add, or do differently except trust that you are enough and move forward, affirming this part of you wholeheartedly with total confidence.

12. Breathe into your heart and make a commitment to honor the wisdom of this part of you. What action could you take, or what practice could you put in place this week to continue moving forward in alignment with what you want to create? Jot down a few notes in your journal.

13. As you complete this exercise, notice if you feel calmer, more empowered, or have more clarity on how to proceed forward.

Your work is to consciously pay attention and notice when the voice of your not-good-enough self is attempting to sabotage you and instead, shift your view of this part of you. Begin to see this part of you as an ally, as having wisdom and guidance that will help you fulfill your dreams and create what you desire.

THE VOICE OF YOUR NOT-GOOD-ENOUGH SELF

I know that giving your not-good-enough self a voice may feel counterintuitive, like you are giving this part of you more power and more energy. But the truth is that the more we squelch the expression of our not-good-enough self, the more we resist what it's trying to communicate, the more we suppress it back into the shadows of our psyche, the louder the voice becomes. It can literally feel like it's taking on a life of its own. If you have ever heard the persistent, negative internal dialogue interrupt you as you attempt to think positively or state affirmations, you know exactly what I'm talking about.

There is the part of you that believes in you and wants to be positive and encouraging dueling the part of you that doesn't feel good enough, that is continually highlighting all the reasons why what you want isn't possible. By giving your not-good-enough self a voice, letting your not-good-enough self scream at the top of his or her lungs, you honor the expression of this part of you and can gain the wisdom that is present. Remember, there's a reason you don't feel enough, and connecting with this part of you will give you that insight. So instead of fighting against it, you will be able to see this newfound wisdom as a gift.

You can find peace knowing that this is just a part of who you are—a part of every human being. As we have explored, each one of us has a part of us that doesn't feel good enough, that feels like we don't measure up in some way in some area of our lives. Although you may not admire or like this part of you, your goal is not to get rid of this part of you or diminish its voice—it is simply to make peace with it. To no longer allow it to be the judge and jury or the director of your life.

Once you honor it, once you let it out, this part of you will no longer have a hold on you. You will feel a sense of peace. You will be able to move forward in alignment with what you want to create in your life.

In addition, by viewing this part of you as an ally instead of an antagonist, you will be able to gain the message this part of you holds—wisdom that can help you fulfill your dreams and create what you desire. For example, let's say that you are writing a book and you start to feel that what you're writing isn't good enough. Instead of letting this part of you be the judge and jury and have you doubt yourself and give up your writing, thereby determining your destiny, give this part of you a voice like you did with the exercise above so you can identify what is truly going on. Instead of staying stuck, you will then be empowered to move forward, take action, and fulfill your desires.

BITE-SIZE EXERCISE

***

Take a few minutes right now to write down what the part of you that doesn't feel good enough or feels inadequate has stopped you from doing or experiencing in your life. Maybe it's kept you from writing a book, starting a new business, changing your job or career, or trusting that you can find a partner who genuinely loves you for who you are. Identifying what your not-good-enough self has kept you from doing will give you insight into what you may want to reconsider embarking upon at some point in your life. Once you are more connected to your 'more-than-enough, you've-got-this, go-for-it' self, your confidence will soar, and you will be equipped with the energy you need to move forward on what is important to you in your life.

In the next chapter, you will continue to deepen your relationship with the part of you that feels more than enough by indulging in how unique, amazing, talented, and truly magnificent you are.

Get ready. We are taking feeling *more than enough* to a whole new level in chapter 5.

5

INDULGE IN HOW UNIQUE YOU ARE

You are brilliant enough, talented enough,
courageous enough, and powerful enough to fulfill
your life's purpose and live your best life.

You are special. You are powerful. You are unique. You are loved.

There is not one being on this planet who can contribute your gift in the same way you can. Every experience you have had, both good and bad, has left a special imprint on your soul and is the divine formula that makes you *uniquely you.* That's how special and magnificent you are. You were sent here on a unique mission that only you can fulfill.

For a moment sit with that truth. Indulge in it. Get present to it. Think about how powerful and life affirming that is. There is not one being on this planet like you. Not one. Take a moment to breathe that in. Indulge in what it feels like to acknowledge this truth. Know that everything you desire can be yours by staying connected to the part of you that believes in you and knows you are *more than enough* to fulfill your life's purpose and live your best life.

Take a moment right now to affirm this by repeating this to yourself seven times as you breathe it into every cell of your being:

"I am brilliant enough, talented enough, courageous enough, and powerful enough to fulfill my life's purpose and live my best life."

Whatever has made you feel less than this truth has simply been a part of societal conditioning, something you internalized at some point in your life, or was a part of your upbringing in some way. You can choose to reject all of that now and reconnect to the truth of who you truly are.

This may feel a bit unattainable to you, or it may feel like it's simply not possible at all. That I can understand. But think about this for a moment. If your heart's desires are aligned with your highest self, are arising from the depth of your soul, and are part of your life's purpose, why wouldn't you be able to create what you desire?

For a moment sit with that. Get present to it. Think about how empowering that is.

Reflect upon how you feel when you ask yourself this question:

If my heart's desires are aligned with my highest self, are arising from the depth of my soul, and are part of my life's purpose, why wouldn't I be able to create what I desire?

As I ask myself that question, it makes me feel more hopeful, more alive, like more possibilities are available. How does it make you feel?

The mission of this chapter is to get you to the place where you are not only pondering this truth but also believing it in the depth of your soul, and most importantly, acting on it wholeheartedly in your life. The following exercise will kickstart your connection to believing this to be truer than you may have a few moments ago.

RECONNECT TO YOUR LIGHT & CONFIDENCE EXERCISE

Find a quiet place to do this visualization. Then close your eyes, and take a slow, deep breath and follow that breath inside, noticing the rise and fall of your chest and your abdomen.

1. As you take a few slow deep breaths, call up a time when you felt confident, on top of your game, alive, brilliant, or uniquely you. Recall a time when you felt loved, adored, or valued.

2. As you reconnect with this memory, take a moment to jot down the vivid details of where you were, what was happening, and how you felt about yourself.

3. Take a few moments right now to envision what you looked like and what your life was like. As you continue to reconnect to how it felt, recognize that even though you may be older or in a different phase of your life, this is still you. You can still connect with the confidence, energy, power, and brilliance you possessed.

4. Breathe into those feelings. Feel them in every cell of your being. Let this memory guide you into connection with the feelings of confidence, self-love, self-respect, freedom, joy, peace, faith, trust, or whatever you may need right now.

5. Take a deep breath and own who are. Own that you created what you are envisioning right now. Own that you are magnificent and unique. Acknowledge that just like you created that amazing experience, you can create something new in your life by accessing these same feelings, by connecting with these qualities at any time. Allow yourself to see how reconnecting to your confidence, your strength, your brilliance, your uniqueness, or whatever is arising for you will help you accomplish what you most desire right now in your life.

6. Take a moment to jot down some notes about what you are envisioning—the way you look, the way you feel, the energy you emanate.

7. Then write down one action you are committed to taking over the next seven days that is in alignment with bringing

more of this energy into every action you take, into creating your life the way you want it to be.

8. Make a commitment for the next seven days to reconnect with this memory, to envision yourself at your best. Your work every morning is to spend a few minutes reconnecting to this younger version of yourself and bringing the energy of this part of you into everything you do.

I hope you felt the power of recalling that amazing moment. This memory and the energy surrounding it is always available to you. Anytime you choose to, you can simply close your eyes and reconnect with this special memory and indulge in these empowering feelings. Allow them to reconnect you to your uniqueness, your magnificence, your greatness. Allow them to connect you with the knowing that just like then, you are still confident, brilliant, unique, and powerful. You haven't lost any of these attributes or qualities, even though you may have disconnected from them for a while. Take a moment to acknowledge that you are the same person today who created that experience then. As you do the work to reconnect to this truth, to this knowing, you will have more access to the energy you need to create what you desire in your life.

RECONNECT TO YOUR LIGHT & CONFIDENCE IN ACTION

Let's look at this exercise and how I use this method of reconnecting to my light, my brilliance, and my confidence as a source of inspiration and the knowing that anything is possible, especially when I am feeling a bit unmotivated, less than inspired, or am lacking confidence.

One of the most amazing, life-defining moments I had was shortly after *Clarity* was published. I was invited to do a segment on ABC7 news in Los Angeles with Denise Dador about forgiveness. All of chapter 7 of my first book, *Clarity*, was devoted to how to forgive when you have been hurt or wronged. To say this was a monumental moment in my life would be an understatement.

We shot the three-minute-long segment at about ten in the morning. It was quite energizing, fast-paced, somewhat of a whirlwind. It took approximately three hours to shoot the entire thing. The brilliant and talented reporter, Denise Dador, guided the entire process and asked powerful questions. The cameraman placed us in many different scenes and took what felt like an immense amount of video. It was both exhilarating and a bit nerve-racking as it was the first time I had done anything like this.

Fast-forward to a few hours later in my dear friend's living room where we were waiting to watch the segment. It was set to air at some point during the five o'clock news. I remember feeling anxious as I sat on the edge of her couch and waited. My friend's husband and her mom were also there, and we were chitchatting as we waited.

As the show began, the anchors and reporters were talking about local happenings. And then I heard the anchor start talking about forgiveness and *I knew that this was it.* This was the moment I got to see it all come together. I perked up on the edge of my seat and watched in awe as three hours of filming turned into a powerful three-minute story of transformation and forgiveness that highlighted my new book, *Clarity*, and the wisdom I shared as a life coach. Watching it all come together was such a glorious moment, and to have them there to celebrate with me was the icing on the cake.

Just as significant as the powerful message of the segment was the reality that this was the first time I saw myself on TV. It was an out-of-body experience, and I'm sure I was lit up watching it. What made it even more special was a dear friend of mine who was one of my mentors and a huge supporter of my work, sent me a text at that very moment. "I'm so proud of you," she said. "I had no idea you were going to be on ABC7 news today, and I was in the kitchen when it came on, thought I heard your voice, and flipped around to see your shining face. You did amazing!"

I can tell this story and relive it like it was yesterday as I have thought about it often over the past five years. I have stayed connected to this monumental moment and have looked back on it many times since it occurred as a source of inspiration, confidence, and the knowing that anything is possible. It is also a beautiful reminder to me that anything worth achieving takes an immense amount of dedication, time, energy, and focus. That experience, that moment in time, did not come easily. It was decades in the making and was only possible through years and years of hard work, and most significantly, a belief in myself.

It's also just as important, given what we are talking about in this book, to share that this, however, is only part of the story. A few weeks later, I was on another TV show and in my view, it was a bit disastrous. I didn't sleep the night before, and I just wasn't "on" during the segment. It was taped in front of a live audience in real time, so editing the show was not an option. Although I obviously remember that TV moment as well, it was not a great one. I am intentionally mindful to not call up that memory often as it can awaken the feeling of not being good enough and could deter me from doing future TV interviews, which isn't aligned with sharing what I have to say.

MEGAN'S CATASTROPHIC BREAKUP

One of the reasons people seek me out as a life coach is to deepen their belief in themselves, to feel more confident, and to achieve what they desire. It can be easy, as we've highlighted throughout this book, to lose confidence in ourselves at different points in our lives. Or to use a not-so-great-moment, like the second TV show I did, to beat ourselves up, to believe something damaging or detrimental about our talent or our ability. Life's not easy—it can take a toll on our self-esteem, and it can definitely beat us down. This is exactly what was happening to my client, Megan, a fifty-eight-year-old interior decorator.

She started working with me because her confidence had been catastrophically rocked by her recent breakup. Megan's relationship had recently had a disastrous ending. Fifteen years of love, connection, and building their life together were suddenly over. She felt a myriad of opposing emotions. There was sadness, a huge void, and a bit surprising to her, a huge desire to do something different, something out of the box. Her relationship, although comfortable in many ways, had left her feeling like she had been complacent for years, like she was often going through the motions, like she had lost the fire she once had. She shared with me that she was ready to find herself again.

She had always dreamed of having her own interior decorating business, and the breakup was the impetus she needed to take the leap and give it a shot. Her job working for one of the top design companies in the city, like her relationship, had been an area of her life that just wasn't in alignment with who she was anymore. Her boss was extremely difficult and stressful to deal with, and she knew she could make more money on her own. So she gave her two-weeks' notice, and with her newfound freedom, she decided to launch the business she had always wanted to start.

There was a part of her that knew she could do it—that was the exhilarating part. But there was also a part of her that was worried she wasn't good enough, that she wasn't unique enough to really make it a go, and it was starting to paralyze her from being able to make big decisions and take action.

This is where our powerful work together began. Learning about Megan's childhood and the challenges and successes of her life was instrumental in determining the direction we would take in our sessions. Once I knew that Megan had created success in her life despite having a challenging upbringing, the key was to reconnect her to that confidence, to those empowering feelings, to the qualities she already possessed that had catapulted her to achieve success in her late twenties. To reconnect her to the knowing that she was still creative, energetic, and confident. Now, just as she had done back then, she could create success in her life. Even though life had taken a toll on her, even though she was worn down and exhausted from a critical, demanding boss and a heartbreaking end to her relationship, she could rise again and step into the brilliant, powerful, creative being she knew herself to be.

In our first session, I guided her to connect with the younger version of herself who had created success as a brand-new interior decorator at the very first company she worked for in her late twenties.

"What does she look like, and what energy does

she emanate?" I asked. Megan told me that she looked alive, vibrant, unstoppable. I could feel the energy in Megan's voice.

"Ask her to tell you how it felt to be recognized as the up-and-coming interior decorator right out of college," I said.

Megan looked into the eyes of the younger version of herself and listened. This is what she heard and what she shared with me.

She was a firecracker. I can feel the drive she had. She had it rough, yes. But she always had an inner fire, a desire to make it, a desire to prove that she was brilliant, talented, and successful just like her dad was. She adored her dad, and although she didn't get to spend much time with him, she looked up to him. She always dreamed of, one day, being as successful as he was.

I invited Megan to stay connected to the power she felt, to the confidence that this younger version of herself wholeheartedly emanated. By reconnecting to her, Megan would be able to draw on this energy anytime she wanted to.

Megan's work every morning before she went into her home office was to reconnect to this younger version of herself, the twenty-seven-year-old who created success shortly out of college. To remember how ingenious she was, how alive she felt, and reconnect to the knowing that although she was older and wiser, she still possessed the qualities she needed to be successful, this time, in her very own business endeavor.

You may not aspire to start your own interior design business, be on TV, or write a book. Your aspirations may be much different. Each one of our journeys is as unique as our DNA. Whatever you want to create in your life, whatever your purpose may be, it is not only possible but attainable by believing in yourself. By knowing that if it is aligned with your highest self, is arising from the depth of your soul, and is part of your life's purpose, with hard work, perseverance, and consistent action, you can create what you desire.

Take a few minutes to do the following bite-size exercise to solidify what we've worked on in this chapter.

BITE-SIZE EXERCISE

***

Anytime you feel insecurity, fear, or self-doubt arise, anytime you feel it begin to fill your thoughts with reasons to not move forward, lessen your commitment, or quit altogether, reconnect to this truth by standing in front of the mirror, looking deeply into your eyes, and saying this aloud:

"I am brilliant enough, talented enough, courageous enough, and powerful enough to fulfill my life's purpose and live my best life."

Then repeat this three more times throughout the day.

Remember, it takes time to encode your mind with positive thoughts that will inspire you and lift you up. It takes time to develop a deep connection with the part of you that feels more than enough and believes in you. Be patient with yourself and stay consistent. You will see a change in how you feel and what you are able to create in your life over time as a result.

I hope it's starting to feel nothing short of amazing to learn new ways to connect with your more-than-enough self and to see more possibilities for your life from this newfound connection to the part of you that believes in you and is always cheering you on. In the next chapter, we will dive into one of the biggest obstacles you may encounter on the journey to staying connected to your more-than-enough self and creating your best life, and that is self-doubt. In addition, we will dive into my three-step formula for success that can serve as both a guide and a blueprint for staying on track in the pursuit of your biggest dreams and the creation of your best life.

6

THE
SABOTAGING
NATURE OF
SELF-DOUBT

Self-doubt is, ultimately, a disconnection from your truth, your greatness, your soul.

Let's have a heart-to-heart, a moment to talk straight. I have some good news and maybe not-so-great news.

Although you've done a lot of work connecting to your more-than-enough self, the likelihood that you are going to soar off into the sunset and be blissful from this point forward is a bit slim.

The truth is you will never get rid of the part of

you that doesn't feel enough. You may want to read that again and let it sink in. *You will never get rid of the part of you that doesn't feel good enough.*

However, the good news is that you can continue to get intimately connected to the voice of this part of you and the ways in which your not-good-enough self shows up or tries to steal the show so that it doesn't catch you off guard or take over without you realizing what is happening. In this chapter, we will take a deep dive into one of the ways our not-good-enough self tries to stop us from achieving what we desire, and that is through the voice of *self-doubt*.

If you have ever questioned yourself after you've said something or replayed an event in your mind repeatedly, you've experienced self-doubt.

It can sound like:

- Was it OK to say that?
- I don't think she likes me.
- Why do I always do *that*?
- What if he was offended by what I said?
- What if he leaves me?
- What if she doesn't talk to me anymore?

Self-doubt can also be a dream killer on the journey to creating our best life and can sound like:

- I don't know if I have what it takes.
- I don't have it in me anymore.
- I'm not as confident, smart, attractive, wealthy, etc., as she is.
- I don't know *how* to do this.
- I don't know *what* to do.
- What if I spend all this time and can't make this work?

I too know exactly what it feels like to have self-doubt arrive on the scene and try to steal the show. Three weeks before my first book, *Clarity*, was set to be released, I began to doubt myself. Yes, yet again.

Truth be told it is quite a miracle that the book ever got published. After years of sweat, tears, writing, editing, and finally seeing the book to completion, the fear of being exposed crept in and hit me like a ton of bricks one day. I was terrified to share the intimate details of how it felt to grow up in the dysfunction of an alcoholic family. To have it published in a book that would be forever out there. So, after all the work I had done, I toiled with not allowing it to be published.

The publisher never knew this. My publicist, at the time, didn't know either. I sat with this privately for an extraordinarily long, grueling seven days.

87

As I shared in chapter 1, the part of me that didn't feel good enough almost kept me from initially sending the manuscript to my dear friend who was previously in the book publishing business. And now, once again, the self-doubt that was arising from the part of me that didn't feel strong enough or courageous enough was attempting to put a kibosh on this book once again, less than three weeks before it would be sitting on the shelf at Barnes & Noble.

This time it was heavier, much more debilitating, and overtook my entire being in a way that sitting in the car that day holding my manuscript didn't.

So what did I do? How did I escape this near disaster and fend off self-doubt this time around?

I worked through it by facing it head on. By connecting with myself, my fear, and the little girl within me who was backpedaling, panicking, and feeling an immense amount of terror and self-doubt. I gave myself permission to be present with what I was truly feeling: not strong enough and not courageous enough to be that vulnerable, to expose myself in that way.

Remember, when we allow ourselves to get present to how we are feeling and what we are experiencing, we give ourselves the space we need to process through what's really going on. From this place, we are then open to gain the wisdom of what our resistance is here to teach us.

Here's the dialogue I had with the little girl within me who was feeling fear and self-doubt:

"Just breathe. It's OK. You don't have to do this. You don't have to publish this book," I said.

"Good. I don't want to. I'm good. I'm healed. I don't need to share the intimate details of my life," said the little girl within me who was terrified of being exposed. "I've experienced enough pain in my life. I don't need to be humiliated by having this book forever out there."

"Yes. I understand how you feel, and I'm OK with this book not being published. I'm here to protect you and won't allow you to be humiliated anymore," I said to reassure her. I did truly feel that it was essential to give myself permission to not publish that book and instead honor how I felt and what I needed.

I then went on to say to the terrified little girl within me, "What's the worst that can happen?"

"People will know the intimate details of my life.

I am a private person, and I don't want that. And worse, what if people don't like it? What if it's a huge flop?" asked the little girl.

"Uh huh. Yes. That's definitely a possibility," I said. I continued, "And what if that happens? Will you be able to love yourself through it like you have with so many other things that have been heart-wrenching in your life?"

"I guess," said the little girl reluctantly.

I then began to shift into connecting with the gift of publishing the book by saying, "What if this book helps one person who has experienced trauma like you did? Would it be worth it to take that risk?"

I sat with this question for a few days. I didn't push myself. I didn't force the little girl within me to do anything other than be with the power of this question.

What happened one morning was nothing short of miraculous. I woke up and knew that I was OK. I was more than OK. I was excited about having *Clarity* published.

By connecting with my inner child, by validating the little girl within me who was terrified, by easing her concerns and being with what I was feeling, by allowing myself the space to simply be, the fear and panic dissipated, and I woke up that day connected to my deeper truth: I did need to share my story. It was part of my healing. It was part of my life's purpose. And, as I shared in chapter 1, it was an essential part of my journey because *Clarity* helped thousands of people heal, reclaim their light, create success in their lives, forgive past hurts, and heal difficult relationships.

Self-doubt can be extremely debilitating. Most of us know what it feels like to flip-flop back and forth through being powerfully connected to our truth and greatness one minute, forging ahead wholeheartedly in our life, and the next moment allowing self-doubt and fear to instantaneously turn our motivation and inspiration upside down, rapidly careening us back to the shores of safety and familiarity.

I'm going to assert that the journey of life is this experience over and over again— the weaving back and forth from our highest, most evolved self to our lowest, most wounded self and stopping off at many different destinations in between. This very flip-flopping back and forth, as well as allowing self-doubt to stop her from finishing her book, was the reason Amanda began sessions with me.

AMANDA'S SELF-DOUBT DEFAULT

Amanda, a forty-two-year-old freelance journalist, came to our session feeling both exhilarated and terrified about the book she was working on. She was proud of herself for continuing to take action toward completing her first book but was extremely frustrated by how quickly self-doubt would take over and steal weeks of time, focus, and dedication.

The self-doubt, once it took hold, was so debilitating that many times she considered not completing the book at all. She shared that this project was becoming so overwhelming that it was all she thought about, and it was causing her a lot of anxiety.

As she shared with me how she was feeling, I knew that not only was she stuck in fear and self-doubt, but she was rarely able to bring the depth of her wisdom into her writing because the emotional chaos was getting in the way and was bleeding into her work.

It was causing her to stop and start, dive in and quit hours later, and sometimes just avoid writing altogether. If she kept up this noncommittal back and forth, she was never going to see this book through to completion.

I gave her a practice that would help her to transcend self-doubt. To retrain herself to focus on the good instead of the negative, to fill herself up instead of breaking herself down. To no longer allow the self-doubt that arose to determine what was possible for her and her life, and most significantly, to no longer come between her and her goal of becoming a published author.

EXERCISE

YOUR TURN: TRANSCEND SELF-DOUBT

Find a quiet place to do this visualization. Close your eyes, and take a slow, deep breath, and follow that breath inside noticing the rise and fall of your chest and your abdomen. Take a few slow, deep breaths, and then begin the exercise.

1. Think of a project you are working on or something you want to accomplish. As you bring that goal into focus, take a few moments right now to identify the ways you attack yourself, judge yourself, criticize yourself, make yourself wrong, or make it

hard to accomplish what you desire by listening to the negative voice you hear in your head. It may sound like, *"I can't do this. I won't follow through. I'm not going to succeed, so why bother? It's too much work. What if I fail? I'm too old. I'm not smart enough, I'm not [fill in the blank] enough."* What are the ways that you break yourself down or make it hard to accomplish what you desire?

2. Next, remember that every time you judge, criticize, attack, make yourself wrong, or beat yourself up, you are doing that to the little girl or little boy within you. Picture that precious child right now.

3. Spend time loving your inner child right now by telling her how sorry you are that you have made things hard for her, that you have been mean to her, that you have judged her or continually beat her up. See her sitting in front of you, and as you look into her eyes, let her know you are learning new ways to love her, care for her, and encourage her, instead of breaking her down and making her feel bad.

4. Every day for the next seven days, your work is to write out five entries in your journal for each one of these three

94

categories below and say them either silently or aloud with the intention of filling yourself up with love and encouragement.

- Category one: *Focus on what is working and going well.* Instead of focusing on what is not working in your life, focus on what is going well.
- Category two: *Focus on your gifts and uniqueness.* Instead of focusing on what you're not great at, focus on your gifts, what makes you unique, and what you're doing well.
- Category three: *Focus on what you love about yourself.* Instead of focusing on what you don't like about yourself, focus on what you love about yourself.

Take some time right now to write these three categories in your journal and begin this process. Be intentional about filling yourself up with love and encouragement, today and every day, moving forward.

A CLIENT JOURNAL ENTRY:

1. Category One: There is so much chaos in my job, and it's causing me a lot of anxiety. Instead of giving this anxiety a lot of attention, I am going to focus on what is going well. I have a job and I'm really good at what I do. I am grateful for the parts of it that I love, and I'm learning new ways to deal with the chaos and anxiety that I feel.

2. Category Two: I can easily get distracted and overwhelmed. Instead of getting completely frustrated with myself, I will focus on how brilliant I am at what I do and be patient with myself.

3. Category Three: When I look at myself in the mirror, all I see is my big nose and it makes me feel bad every single time. Instead of looking at my nose, I am going to switch my focus. The next time I look in the mirror, I will look at my beautiful soulful eyes instead, letting them fill me up with the depth of who I really am.

ANOTHER CLIENT JOURNAL ENTRY:

1. Category One: My relationship is a disaster, and it makes me feel like a failure.

I just can't seem to get this part of my life right. Instead of beating myself up for this, I am going to focus on how much better I am treating myself. I know that over time, as I treat myself with more love and respect, my relationship will mirror that love.

2. **Category Two:** I have never been good at saying nice things to myself. It is literally a struggle every day. Instead of feeling discouraged, I am going to notice how much I have created in my life despite my ability to talk to myself kindly. I'm working on this diligently right now and will keep getting better at it day by day.

3. **Category Three:** I get really frustrated with myself because I am so disorganized. Instead of focusing on the disorder and beating myself up, I am going to acknowledge how creative and talented I am. It's a talent in and of itself to be able to complete amazing creative projects even though my office and my desk are a perpetual mess.

By consciously choosing what you are focusing

on and giving your precious energy to, you will continually build the muscles of self-love and self-encouragement instead of letting self-doubt and self-criticism take over and limit what is possible for you.

LOVINGLY RETRAIN YOURSELF

The truth is that many of us are extremely hard on ourselves. Like I shared in chapter 1, I have had the honor of coaching people for the past twenty years and have witnessed the debilitating, destructive ways self-doubt can keep the greatest, most unique human beings from acknowledging their unique nature, fulfilling their purpose, and living their best life.

The good news is that the damage that has been done is not permanent. On any given day, in any moment, we have the power to change what we're focusing on and how we are talking to ourselves. We can either build the muscle of self-encouragement and self-love, encouraging it to blossom and grow, or we can allow self-doubt to fester and take us down by continuing to harshly judge and criticize ourselves.

As you embark on this journey of retraining yourself, be gentle.

Remind yourself that it is a process. It takes time to retrain ourselves to focus on the good instead of the negative. To fill ourselves up instead of breaking ourselves down. To believe in our uniqueness instead of diminishing our greatness. But it is worth every amount of energy you give it. It is one of the most important things you can do for yourself every single day from this point forward.

INFUSE ENERGY EXERCISE

One of my true and tested ways to step into feeling good enough when self-doubt arises is to infuse my day with what I have already accomplished.

I will take time to look back, to indulge, to fill myself up, to remind myself of what I have already created, where I have come from, how far I've traveled, and who I have become.

I might read rave reviews of one of my previous books or look back at testimonials of people who have coached with me. I may look at a photo of my daughter and husband, the two people I adore and am grateful to spend my life with, watch a video of my daughter shining her light, or remind myself of monumental moments in my life where I showed up powerfully and made a difference.

Each time you do this for yourself, it awakens the truth about who you are. It quiets that voice inside you that says you're not enough, and it inspires you to forge ahead in your life from the part of you that is powerful, wise, and knows who you truly are and what you are here to contribute in your lifetime.

Right now, take out your journal and spend five to ten minutes writing down what you have accomplished over the past five to ten years. How you have grown. Who you have become.

After you finish writing, notice how you feel. Do you feel proud of yourself, filled up, inspired? Maybe you feel more fulfilled, joyful, or at peace. Or maybe you have had a tough few years and are finding it hard to see something positive about what you have accomplished. Look deeply. Start small. Look for one thing you feel good about, one thing you are proud of. Look at what you have survived. Every little encouragement we give ourselves builds our self-esteem and becomes the energy that will continue to catapult us into creating more of what we desire.

Imagine the positive energy that would awaken within you if you made this a daily practice. Imagine what you could not only create in your life as a result but also how amazing you would feel along the way.

AN ESSENTIAL CAVEAT

There is one caveat. One important distinction I must share that is crucial to keep in mind.

Although I'm suggesting that you connect with your accomplishments and what you feel good about in your life as a pathway into the part of you that feels *enough*, accomplishments and creating success are not what ultimately makes you feel good enough.

What solidifies the belief that you are enough comes from a knowing in the depths of your soul. Just because you are *you*, you are enough. When you were born you were enough. You are still enough, regardless of what has happened in your life.

My hope is that everything I am guiding you to do will return you to this knowing, return to the truth of who you are. To a state of wholeness that once reclaimed can never be lost. And although you may feel disconnected from this knowing at various times throughout your life, it is always there awaiting your return.

You may be struggling a bit with this truth or wondering, like one of my recent clients, what makes you worthy. You may have more doubt or uncertainty than a solid knowing at this moment. You may be able to relate to my recent client, Dena, a thirty-nine-year-old executive assistant, who just could not grasp her own worth. Life had broken her down so much that she truly didn't believe that she was worthy for any reason, in any way. She was so hard on herself, so critical, that it was almost impossible for her to be kind and loving to herself, to give herself the same grace and compassion she gave to others.

DENA'S RISE TO GRACE AND COMPASSION

In Dena's first session, we began the process of unraveling why she had such low self-esteem and was so hard on herself. I asked her to tell me about her childhood because so much of who we are originates from our younger years.

"I was a difficult child," she said. "My mom used to tell me how selfish I was. I don't know why I could not do what was required of me like my sister did. But I couldn't. I remember my mom always criticizing the things I said, the way I acted, who I was. I'm not sure why I was so difficult all the time,

MORE THAN ENOUGH

I guess I was just a bad kid. The truth is I am still difficult to deal with. I have continued throughout my adulthood to act out in relationships, always creating a mess, like I did as a child."

Listening to Dena criticize herself was tough. It was heartbreaking to hear how little she thought of herself, to hear her say that she truly felt she was flawed as a child.

I tried to reassure her that every child acts out at times and doesn't behave perfectly. It's a part of learning, it is a part of growing up. Even adults do the wrong thing at times. After all, we are human. But that did not seem to register with Dena. She still felt at her core that she was flawed and didn't deserve grace. She kept reiterating that it was her fault that her mom was so critical of her. That there was something wrong with her.

Sometimes our wounds are so deep, so suppressed, that it's hard to get connected to where the wound originated from. That was exactly what was happening for Dena. She was trying to make sense of why she was such a *bad* child despite her parents providing for her. So, to deal with her lack of understanding, she made up a story about herself that she felt she could wrap her brain around even though it wasn't based on the truth.

Unfortunately, the story she made up was

103

extremely painful and damaging to her sense of worth and her well-being. The good news, however, was that the part of her that knew she was worthy was still alive and well. Although you couldn't hear a trace of that part of her when she spoke about herself, I knew it was still present because otherwise she would not be working with me. She would not have sought out coaching to help her unravel this pain so that it no longer defined her. She would have instead resigned herself to being miserable and feeling horrible about herself. And that would have been the end of the story. But it wasn't.

Nonetheless, the work Dena did in our sessions wasn't easy, and as is usually the case, we ran into a bit of resistance. Dena had a tough time reckoning with the reality that her mom's parenting style had been part of why she felt bad about herself. She had a tough time looking at her mom's shortcomings. I had to reassure her that we weren't doing this to blame or criticize her mom. It wasn't for the sole purpose of pointing the finger at her mom or deflecting Dena's responsibility for her actions. But the reality is she was a child. She was learning. And she deserved to make mistakes on the journey to learning right and wrong without being shamed and made to feel like she was a bad kid. It was important to look at and identify the way Dena had internalized her mother's criticism, the way her mother shamed her for acting the way she did, and what Dena had made it mean about her.

Remember, there is a reason people act the way they do. It doesn't in any way deflect personal responsibility. However, it's important to look at the whole picture. The truth is that when we are born, we are whole. Then life can take a toll, beat us down, and create a fracture in the foundation of our worth, which can stay etched in our psyche for a long time.

Three decades later, Dena was still criticizing herself the way her mom did. It was all she knew. It was who she believed herself to be. Her work in our sessions helped her to break through this false sense of self and reconnect to her greatness, to her innocence, to her sweet soul that was worthy of love just because she was inherently worthy. She did not have to behave a certain way to be worthy. There didn't need to be a reason for her to be worthy of love. She simply was.

The work Dena embarked on in our sessions reconnected her to her soul, to her greatness, to her worth. Week after week, and month after month, she showed up to our weekly session and she did the work to unravel the layers of criticism and judgment, to release the shame that had whittled away her sense of self and her self-esteem. Every week, she saw more of her light, her sweetness, her innocence, her worth peeking out from within. It was nothing short of miraculous to watch.

Whatever you have experienced, whatever trauma has caused you to feel like you are not good enough or worthy of love, doesn't have to continue to define you. You have the power, just like Dena, to unravel and unpack your past so that it no longer limits what is possible for you.

Take a few minutes right now to deepen what you have worked on in this chapter by doing the following bite-size exercise.

BITE-SIZE EXERCISE

***

When you start to feel self-doubt steal the show and tempt you to give up, don't despair. Simply recognize that it is coming from the wounded part of you that doesn't feel good enough. Remind yourself that this is just a part of you, it is not who you are in totality and that there is a reason you are feeling insecure and doubting yourself. This recognition alone will give you time to pause and reconsider. It will give you a moment to identify the fear that is threatening to take over and the option to instead reconnect with your more-than-enough, you've-got-this, go-for-it self, so you can move forward in alignment with what is in your highest and best interest.

As we have been exploring, there are many things throughout life's journey that can disconnect us from our truth, from our greatness, from feeling more than enough.

Another one of the enormous obstacles to being grounded in the knowing that you are *more than enough* is comparison. Like self-doubt, comparing ourselves to others is extremely detrimental to our self-esteem and our well-being. It is such a dream killer that the damage it can do, and how to stop beating yourself up in this way, is the focus of the next chapter.

7

THE
DESTRUCTION
OF COMPARISON

Sammi, a thirty-two-year-old photographer, came to our session disgruntled and a bit down. She was in a funk lately and tired of continually trying to pep herself up and look on the bright side. "I wake up in a bad mood pretty much every day, and getting myself motivated is starting to feel like a part-time job," she said.

Because we had been working together for a few weeks at this point, I knew what was bothering her. She wanted to have a baby, and their attempts at getting pregnant had failed.

"All my friends are having kids, and every time I go on social media, I am inundated with ultrasound photos, first birthday party reels, and the cute outfit that my best friend bought her newborn at babyGap. I mean seriously, the onesie with the navy babyGap baseball cap. I just can't take it anymore. It just leaves me feeling inadequate and deflated."

Enter comparison, the insidious mood deflater.

Maybe you can relate. It's a beautiful Saturday. So far, you're having a pretty decent morning. You just had a cup of coffee, John Mayer is playing in the background, and the sun is shining. This morning you're feeling pretty optimistic and have a few things you need to check off on your to-do list. But instead of starting your day, you decide to procrastinate for a few minutes and jump on social media.

You do a bit of scrolling, nothing that interesting, still scrolling, still nothing much, and then *boom*. One of your friends just posted the most heartfelt photo that consisted of her husband planting a huge smooch on her cheek and giving her a gorgeous bouquet of flowers. And, by the way, he gave her this gesture of love for no apparent reason at all.

In the post, she writes detail after detail about how amazing her husband is, the beautiful things he says to her every day, and how lucky she is to have married him seventeen years ago. You know her words ring true because her husband is pretty fantastic.

Now, given that you love your friend, and under normal circumstances, this might not hit you so hard in the heart, or truth be told, punch you in the gut. You are even a little bit embarrassed that you're feeling this way since this is your friend. But the truth is you have been having a tough time with your husband lately and spending an inordinate amount of time worrying about what is going on with him. He is withdrawn, seems a bit depressed, and the two of you fight more than you ever have before. It's been making you feel a bit insecure, and your biggest fear is that he's not in love with you anymore. To top it off, you've been feeling like the reason he has been withdrawing his love is your fault. You've been feeling so *old* lately. Aging has been tough on you. You have gained a bit more weight than you are comfortable with, and oh yes, the wrinkles, they seem to be spreading like wildfire.

So, because your self-esteem is in the dumps, without even realizing it, you start to compare yourself to your dear friend. Now this innocent photo that she posted an hour ago has ruined your entire morning, in all of five-whole-minutes.

It happens, right? You didn't mean to compare your life to your friend's, but here you are. Feeling envious. Feeling like life's not fair. Wondering what you've done wrong to deserve the heartache you are currently experiencing and why she's always so darn happy.

THE TORTURE OF COMPARISON

Comparing ourselves to others is a part of being human. As we've been exploring, it can be extremely detrimental to our mental and emotional well-being if we use it to make ourselves feel bad. And even more damaging if it stops us from focusing on, tending to, or creating what we want in our own lives.

Think about how extremely unfair it is to compare someone's amazing, picture-perfect moment to a difficult day you're having or a struggle you're facing. And yet, sometimes, we do it anyway. Let's dive into *what's really going on.*

First off, comparing ourselves to others can stem from the part of us that doesn't feel worthy enough, smart enough, attractive enough, courageous enough, successful enough, talented enough, or happy enough. It can be one of the ways that our *not-good-enough self* expresses its insecurity or discontent with our lives.

Nonetheless, let's talk straight. Comparing ourselves to others can be a form of self-torture, a way we either consciously or unconsciously, knowingly or unknowingly, beat ourselves up. And to be clear, the cost of doing this is immense.

Not only can it awaken and heighten the insecurity or discontent we feel, but in addition, when we judge ourselves and compare ourselves to others, we become disconnected from our greatness, our uniqueness, and our ability to enjoy the blessings in our lives. It is that disempowering and detrimental to our well-being and can in a minute or two render us powerless—unless we make a conscious choice to use it as motivation and inspiration to improve our lives, which will dive into later in this chapter.

So, what do you do when you find yourself stuck in the envy, jealousy, or resentment that comparison breeds?

First, it is essential to remind yourself in the moment that you are comparing yourself to someone else, you are now disconnected from your greatness, your unique nature, who you are, and your ability to create what you want in your life. Remind yourself that it's not fair to compare someone's amazing moment to a difficult day you're having or a struggle you're faced with. That is a surefire way to feel bad about yourself. Instead, make the loving choice and commitment to treat yourself with kindness, compassion, and grace.

TIME TO REFLECT

Let's take a deeper dive into exactly what happens in the moment we compare ourselves to someone else so we can not only grasp how damaging it can be but can also understand why we do this in the first place. This insight can give us more compassion for ourselves, inspiration to be gentler with ourselves, and a way out of the grips of comparison.

Take a moment to recall a recent time you remember feeling bad about yourself as you compared your life to someone else's. Maybe it was earlier today or last week. Maybe you heard that critical voice in your head say something like:

Why doesn't my husband say those nice things about me?
Why does she seem to always do everything right?
Why am I still single?
Why can't I have that?
He just got promoted again?
Why does she always look so happy?
Oh my gosh, they are on another vacation?
I wish I could be more...

I wish I were as confident as she is.
I wish my life...

The most important observation you can make when this internal dialogue starts to take hold is that it isn't in your favor, it doesn't make you feel good. Most of the time, it doesn't inspire you, and it can immediately and negatively impact how you feel about yourself and your life. It doesn't affirm who you are or what you are capable of. Let's be honest, it is almost never beneficial.

So, given all that, why do we continue to do this over and over again? And why does it feel almost impossible to refrain from comparing ourselves to others?

One of the reasons is that it is a part of societal conditioning from early on in our lives. From an early age, we are compared to our siblings, to other kids at school, or to kids in our neighborhood. When we begin to get grades and become a part of sports or clubs, comparison can become the way that we judge ourselves and determine whether we are doing enough, whether we measure up to other kids around us.

After all, society values accomplishments. The one who wins often gets the most attention and recognition. That sends a clear message that praise comes to those who achieve. Obviously, this can leave us feeling like we don't measure up at times, and it can breed the feeling of not being good enough.

If this alone isn't enough to solidify our tendency to continually compare ourselves to others, we now have the addition of social media, which is like comparison on steroids. At our fingertips, we have access to what thousands of our so-called friends, colleagues, and even strangers are doing right now in this very moment. As we explored at the beginning of this chapter, if you are not feeling good about yourself or your life when you scroll through your feed, it can be instantaneously disastrous to your self-esteem. It can plunge you into an immediate state of discontent, discouragement, or even despair.

Reflect on this for a moment. How often do you look at a post, reel, or video on social media and think to yourself, "Why can't I do that?" "Why don't I have a spouse who loves me like she does?" "Why isn't my life that fun?" "Why am I not as happy as he is?"

Most of us can relate to having thoughts just like these when we're on social media. And if we are being honest with ourselves, maybe even every single time.

As bleak as this may feel, there is a way out of

this mess. Just like everything else we have talked about in this book, this doesn't have to continue to be your reality. You have the power to make a change by bringing light to this unconscious, habitual behavior. You can shift into a more powerful state of being by consciously and consistently taking actions that are more aligned with your well-being, that are more beneficial to you and your life.

The single most important thing to do in the moment you find yourself comparing yourself to somebody else is to turn your attention and focus back to yourself and get about the business of creating what you want in your life. Stop beating yourself up in this way. Instead, use it as inspiration and motivation. Recognize that when you are envious or jealous, you are seeing something you want to experience in your own life. Let it inspire you. Let it open you up to new possibilities. Let it motivate you into action. Use it as a gift to create something new instead of allowing it to define you or make you feel bad.

Make this commitment to yourself right now. Commit to creating a life that is both inspiring and fulfilling.

Take a deep breath and affirm this truth for yourself by saying it aloud seven times:

*What she is doing has no bearing on my happiness,
how I feel about myself, or what I can accomplish.
Today, I choose to focus on myself and create my life
the way I want it to be.*

In the next section, we will dive into exactly how to get into action, creating more of what you desire every day: more happiness, more freedom, more peace, more fulfillment.

THE PATH TO SUCCESS

The path to success is simple. And I am not just talking about business or career success. I am also referring to experiencing *total* success, which in my definition includes joy, peace, happiness, freedom, and fulfillment.

The path to true success in your life is in following your heart and aligning your life to fulfilling your heart's desires, who you are, and what you are authentically meant to do. While comparing yourself to others can take you away from your unique path, don't fret; by reconnecting to your heart's desires and getting into action, you can rest assured that you will be back on the path to fulfilling your dreams and your highest purpose.

My three-step formula for success is a powerful way to get into action in your life. It will help you identify where you are on the path to success, as well as what you may need to work on to achieve your biggest dreams.

THREE-STEP FORMULA FOR SUCCESS

- **Step One:** Have a strong vision of what you want, and most importantly, keep that vision close to your heart by connecting with it every day. Commit to spending a few minutes each day connecting with what you want to create in your life, envisioning yourself having already accomplished your vision.
- **Step Two:** Take actions that are aligned with your vision, staying both consistent and persistent. This is the step that many people find the most challenging, especially when fear or self-doubt arise. It can be difficult to stay consistent given both the demands of life and our inner turmoil. However, this is an essential component to creating everything we desire, which is why the third step in this formula is also extremely important.

- **Step Three:** Consistently do self-development work. An important part of creating success is to continually embrace your light and greatness and move beyond whatever limitations may get in the way of fulfilling your vision. Make a commitment to not allow self-doubt or fear to stop you. Spend time every day connecting to your strength, courage, power, uniqueness, and the knowing that you can create everything you desire. Listening to these five audio meditations can support you in doing this: www.dianealtomare.com/selflove

As we wrap up our exploration of comparison, remind yourself that comparing yourself to someone else is a part of being human. However, it doesn't have to keep you stuck or keep you from creating what you desire. The next time you find yourself stuck in the self-deprecating energy of comparing yourself to somebody else, take a few minutes to ask yourself these questions:

- Is self-doubt driving me to believe I can't accomplish what I desire?

- Am I not clear on what it is I want to do or who I authentically am?
- Am I not following my heart?
- Is fear clouding my clarity or keeping me from taking action?
- Am I not taking actions that are aligned with the highest vision for my life, my career, and my heart's desires?
- Am I allowing limitations to get in the way of taking consistent action?

Ultimately, you must answer this question:

Am I willing to use this to become stronger and make a deeper commitment to what I want to create in my life, or am I going to allow this to drain my energy and bring me down?

After you reflect on these empowering questions, you may also want to review and reflect on the three-step formula for success as it will help you refocus your energy and attention back toward your life and get you into action creating what you desire.

Remember, your path and journey are unique to you. What someone else is doing has no bearing on your happiness, how you feel about yourself, or what you accomplish. Whenever you find that you're comparing yourself to someone else, simply turn your attention back to yourself and get about the business of creating more of what you want in your life.

Let's look at one of the ways to be more mindful of your well-being while on social media with the exercise below.

BITE-SIZE EXERCISE

***

The next time you are about to jump on social media, use this bite-size exercise to be intentional by taking a moment to first identify how you are feeling. Are you feeling content with yourself and your life? Are you in an upbeat mood, excited about something that is happening later today, or are you feeling a bit down? Set a timer on your phone for ten minutes, jump on social media, and when the timer beeps, ask yourself these questions: How do I feel now? Do I feel inspired? Do I feel grounded? Am I comparing myself to somebody else, or is this draining my energy? Remember that comparing ourselves to someone else is a part of being human. Simply acknowledge this without making yourself feel bad, and then redirect your attention and energy toward focusing on your life and what you want to create for your future.

In the next chapter, we will dive into how easily the part of us that doesn't feel good enough can drive us to be out of balance and what to do to regain your footing when you start to feel off kilter.

8

THE DRIVE TO NEVER ENOUGH

This moment in and of itself is perfect. This moment
is enough, and I am enough.

Have you ever noticed that the moment
you accomplish something, it doesn't take long
to feel the hunger for something more? Something
bigger. Something better. Something you think
will bring you more happiness, more success,
more wealth, more joy.

This is not altogether negative, as there is a
healthy drive within each of us that compels us to
strive, create, evolve, and move beyond our
current circumstances.

However, for some of us, especially those who
have an overdeveloped, highly dysfunctional not-

good-enough self, this force can become all consuming, taking over, kicking us into overdrive, and pushing us until we are exhausted and begging for mercy.

So what do you do when your *drive to achieve* has become a tireless monster, threatening the very peace and happiness you're craving? You pause for a moment, recognize what's happening, take a deep breath, and regain connection to yourself and the desires of your soul. You take time to reflect by asking yourself poignant, self-loving questions.

A few questions to ponder:

- What truly makes me feel fulfilled, happy, and peaceful?
- Is my life set up in a way that gives me space to thrive and to enjoy what I have accomplished?
- Is my inner drive to achieve or my tendency to compare myself to others pushing me to a breaking point? If so, what do I need to let go of or embrace to regain a sense of balance?
- How can I achieve what I desire while at the same time take care of myself and feel peaceful in the process?

As you sit with these questions, recognize that there may be a few adjustments you will need to make to both achieve what you desire and enjoy the journey along the way. While checking things off your to-do list and accomplishing your goals is essential to creating success, it is not the key to a fulfilling and joyous life. Living deeply in the moment and being present to who you are and what you already have *is*.

REBEKAH'S NEVER-ENDING DRIVE TO ACHIEVE

Rebekah, a forty-three-year-old business executive, was a self-proclaimed overachiever desperate to experience less anxiety and more balance in her life. She ran herself ragged most days and found that at the end of the day, although she felt accomplished at work, she had so much anxiety about what was left undone that she couldn't relax with her daughter or enjoy time with her husband.

Some nights, after she put her daughter to bed, she would work until midnight.

"I'm extremely anxious, worried, and stressed out. I may look like I have it all together, but honestly, I'm pretty miserable and stressed out most of the time."

Shortly after Rebekah and I began working together, she began to see how some of the things that happened in her childhood were still negatively impacting her.

Rebekah's dad was hard on her. He didn't praise her much, and worse, seemed to always criticize what she did. When she got a B, he wanted to know what kept her from an A. When she got second place, he assured her that she could've been first if she had worked a little harder. As she shared the details of her relationship with her dad, she was quick to defend him, declaring that he just wanted the *best for her*. But the truth was, the damage his criticism did to her self-esteem and sense of worth was driving her into the ground. It was causing her to miss out on so much in her life.

I invited Rebekah to connect to the little girl within her, the little girl who felt like she was never good enough in her dad's eyes. I guided Rebekah to close her eyes and see that little girl sitting in front of her.

"What does she look like, and how old is she?" I

asked. Rebekah told me that she was five years old and looked terrified, like she was on guard.

"Ask her to tell you how it felt when her dad criticized her," I said.

Rebekah looked into the eyes of that little girl and listened. This is what she heard and what she shared with me.

> I know he loved me. He did. But the truth is I always felt like a disappointment to him and felt like I was fighting for his attention. Whether it was a football game he was watching or work he was doing on his laptop, he never seemed that interested in me or what I was doing. Achieving was how I got his attention, even though he was critical sometimes. He had a rough upbringing. He would always tell me how hard life was, and I think on some level he was tough on me in hopes of preparing me for the hard knocks of life. I remember crying a lot into my pillow at night so he wouldn't hear me. He didn't care much for crying.

I invited Rebekah to stay connected to the little girl's pain, to feel the pain of her dad's continual criticism. I assured her that it would give her clarity and more compassion for the little girl within her who was so exhausted by having to continually achieve to get the tiny little scraps of attention her dad would sometimes hand out. By honoring what that little girl experienced and allowing herself to see how detrimental it was to her self-worth, Rebekah would ultimately be able to give herself the validation and approval that she needed, which she never got from her dad.

In addition to the deep work Rebekah did in her session to heal the little girl who felt inadequate and unlovable, I gave her a practice that would help her to stop giving so much attention and energy to crossing off tasks from her to-do list. Instead of being stuck in overdrive in the pursuit of achieving more success, she would also be able to spend time relaxing and enjoying her life. The All In, All Out exercise that follows is a practice she implemented to help her be more intentional about delineating the time she spent working and the time she wanted to rest and be with her family.

It's a powerful way to practice being 100 percent focused on what you are working on, and 100 percent detached from it when you're not. It allows you to be wholeheartedly intentional about what you are doing when you are focused on it and gives you time to take a break from it when you choose to.

Let's look at how you, too, can use this practice to create more balance in your life.

ALL IN. ALL OUT. PRACTICE

This exercise is exactly what it sounds like. When you are working, you are "all in" and focused on what you are doing. When you are "all out," you intentionally let go of working for that hour, the block of a few hours, or for the rest of the day. A calendar and a timer are essential tools to use for this practice. So grab both and let's begin.

Take out your calendar and block out some time today or over the next few days. For example, allow yourself to simply "be" for a few hours without having to achieve or accomplish anything. Take some time to just let it all go, to set it all down. Turn on a timer for sixty minutes, and take a mental and emotional break from it all. Imagine setting down all your worries, expectations, and concerns so that you can enjoy lunch, a cup of tea, some downtime, or a chat with a friend without the impending thoughts of what you still have left to do threatening your peace of mind.

Be intentional about what you are focusing your energy on by making this declaration:

"I am choosing to set this all down for now and am committed to relaxing and letting go. I will give myself the gift of being deeply present in this moment.

Right here. Right now. This moment in and of itself is enough."

I know this can be easier said than done. That's why we call it a practice. Sometimes, you may be able to let go, relax, and be fully present for only ten minutes of the hour. Other times, longer. And other times, you may not be able to do it at all. But the more you practice intentionally setting down your work and to-do lists and focusing on letting go, relaxing, and enjoying, the easier it will become to do this more often.

One of the ways I have motivated myself to do this, because I, too, am an overachiever, is to remind myself that the more time I spend relaxing, the more focused, intentional energy I can later bring to my work. This alone inspires me to relax more often. I have found that the more energy and time I give to relaxing and recharging my batteries, the more focused, energetic, and calm I feel. There are huge benefits to relaxing and decompressing. It is a beautiful way to balance life, making it much richer and more enjoyable.

ALWAYS OVERWHELMED

Another one of the insidious outcomes of driving yourself to continually achieve more is feeling like you are in a perpetual state of overwhelm. As we have explored, when we feel that we're not enough or what we are accomplishing isn't good enough, that pain or inadequacy can drive us to prove that we *are* enough. It can drive us to a place of working too much and can easily create imbalance in our lives.

Because nothing ever feels like it's enough, it can be hard to say no to the next shiny object or the next project that you hope will bring you more attention, validation, love, success, money, or happiness. The result can be living in a chronic state of overwhelm.

A few of my clients who are continually overwhelmed have shared these sentiments:

- *There is always something going on.*
- *I have a list that never ends. Once something is checked off, something else gets added. It feels like nothing ever gets done.*
- *How am I going to ever find peace or relief from all of this?*
- *I don't know when to quit; I keep going until I'm so exhausted. I can't even relax.*

133

- *I feel like a ping pong ball going from one thing to the next. I have trouble being still.*
- *I feel obsessed with checking my phone.*
- *I don't want to be all over the place like this anymore.*
- *I have a drive to continually achieve. It feels like a battle I am always fighting.*
- *Everything feels insurmountable. There is this weight on my chest, my shoulders; the pressure is almost unbearable at this point.*
- *I'm so stressed, and I just can't relax. I don't know how to turn it off.*
- *I'm physically and mentally exhausted, and the responsibility of it all is just unimaginable.*
- *My heart is beating so fast every moment of the day. I feel like I am constantly running on adrenaline.*
- *I'm always rushing against time. It simply moves too fast.*

Maybe you, too, can relate to feeling this way at times. Perhaps you feel stressed or overwhelmed right now. This, of course, is not ideal and is not a way to live well. Yes, sometimes due to extraordinary circumstances in our lives, we may have to keep up a pace that is unmanageable. However, setting up your life and continuing to work at this pace for a long time is a recipe for disaster. It can both drain your energy and take the joy out of life.

Being overwhelmed means that you have more energy coming at you, more going on in your life than you can comfortably handle. It is simply an overflow of energy that renders you unable to focus and give your undivided attention to any one thing. It keeps you from being present or deeply entrenched in the moment. Ultimately, it is not the way to set up your life if you want to experience success, joy, peace, fulfillment, and happiness. In the end, it is not only detrimental to your well-being and your ability to enjoy your life but you also simply can't bring 100 percent of your focus and attention to what you are doing when you're overwhelmed. Not to mention, things can fall through the cracks and leave you with the overall sense of never doing enough, never being content with the completion of any one thing. Because, well, there is always something else waiting and vying for your time and attention.

AMANDA'S INSATIABLE DRIVE

Amanda, a forty-two-year-old real estate agent, had an addiction to filling up every single waking moment. If she wasn't incessantly checking her phone and her email, she was looking at what she needed to do to cross off the next item on her to-do list.

One of the practices I initially gave her was to pick two hours each day when she could commit to being *away* from her phone. That meant no responding to texts or calls during that time and putting it in a different room in the house than she was in. She picked six to eight o'clock in the evening. Initially, this was tough for her. But she stuck it out and the benefits she shared were instantaneous and nothing short of amazing. She was starting to feel like she had so much more time, more control over her life, and was feeling much calmer.

The moment after she shared that awesome news with me, her addiction to filling up every single moment of her life came alive as she asked me this next question. "Now that I have more time, can I take on the project of remodeling our upstairs bathroom?"

"Uh? Wait, what?" I thought. You can imagine what I said. Yep, you guessed it. I responded with an emphatic no.

She let out a deep belly laugh because she knew she was again being driven by the part of her that wanted to constantly achieve. I went on to say, "Just because you've done an amazing job creating space in your life and now feel like you have more time, your challenge is to *not* fill up this precious space with the next thing on your to-do list or the next project that's waiting. Your challenge is to just let that space be there. Let the space to relax, space to wander, space to do nothing, space to do something for yourself, anything that fills you up and feels good in the moment, space to enjoy all that you have already accomplished, be savored, be protected."

I continued, "Think of your energy like money, like an investment you put into a bank account. Energy in reserves that you can choose to use for something later. You save money in an investment account for your future so that it is there when you need it. Do the same with your energy. Save some of it so that it is in reserve when you need or choose to use it."

Maybe you resonate with Amanda and her addiction to filling up every waking moment or my clients who are in a perpetual state of overwhelm and can't seem to relax. Take a few moments with the following bite-size exercise to identify what you may need to integrate into your daily structure to create more space, more time to relax, more time to enjoy, more time to simply *be*.

BITE-SIZE EXERCISE

***

Take some time right now to create space in your day. Instead of quickly rushing from one task to the next, be intentional about taking time to pause, move slowly, and gather your energy so that you can relax and then wholeheartedly focus on what is next. Simply set a timer for four minutes, close your eyes, and take some slow, deep breaths with the intention of getting present to this moment right here, right now. For the next four minutes, remind yourself that there is nothing to do except let everything go and relax. Follow each inhale and exhale. Let your mind wander. Let yourself be. And then dive into your next task with a renewed sense of energy, calm, and focus.

MY NIGHTTIME RITUAL

In the pursuit of creating new things and accomplishing our goals, it can be easy to hyper-focus on the fifteen things we have not yet achieved. Doing this is often counterproductive, and at times can leave us feeling discouraged and unmotivated. In extreme cases, it can break us down and damage our self-esteem.

It's essential for both your well-being and your ability to create what you desire, to take time each day to remind yourself of what you have already accomplished. This not only gives you fuel and momentum to keep pursuing your goals but it allows you to feel complete, content, fulfilled, and peaceful.

I have a nightly practice before I go to bed where I acknowledge myself for who I am and what I've created, allowing myself the space to be at peace with what already is, even if I never create anything more. It is a way to feel complete with the incompleteness of life. It's also a powerful way to shift toward focusing on what's working and going well instead of always focusing on what is left undone. I have found it to be a beautiful way to end my day.

Here is what I say every night as I let go of the day and rest my head on the pillow:

I honor every single step I took today to fulfill my highest vision and purpose. I am complete. If I never sell another book, have another coaching client, or make another dollar, it is enough, and I am complete. Right now, in this moment, I choose to let it all go. All is well. I am enough. And so it is. And it is so.

For the next few nights, practice acknowledging

yourself for what you have already accomplished. Allow yourself the gift of feeling complete when you lay your head in bed at night or when you've completed working on your project for the day.

Remember, what we focus on expands. So if we are always focusing on what is left undone or what we still have to do, it can create feelings of lack or the feeling that we will never arrive to our destination or achieve our goal. And that just does not feel good. In addition, it can awaken self-doubt or the feeling that nothing is ever enough. On the other hand, if we are continually acknowledging what we are doing well, what we have already accomplished, and who we have become, it solidifies feelings of fulfillment, contentment, and peace.

Want more? Listen as I guide you through the exercise below on audio. Find the audio at www.dianealtomare.com/letting-go-meditation

LETTING GO NIGHTTIME MEDITATION

This is one of my favorite nighttime meditations to let go of the day. I like to do this sitting in front of the fire with a warm cup of almond milk, some nights adding cardamom and cinnamon, and using this as a meditation to let go

and surrender to a peaceful night's sleep. It has become a beautiful ritual to end the day. Find a quiet place to do this visualization. Then close your eyes, take a slow, deep breath, and follow that breath inside, noticing the rise and fall of your chest and your abdomen.

1. As you take a slow, deep breath, give yourself permission to just be here. Feel your hip bones sink into the chair where you are seated. Your feet ground into the earth.

2. Take a moment to notice where your mind may want to take you. To something from your day, perhaps something you must do tomorrow. Just follow that for a moment.

3. Observe how you feel about that thought, that experience, or that person. Give yourself permission to be with whatever you are feeling. Maybe the emotion is heavy, disappointing, or you feel frustrated or resigned to something not going the way you want it to go. Take a moment to let it be as it is. Let yourself feel whatever you are feeling. And then smile to those emotions. Yes, smile to your anger, smile to your upset, smile to the pain you may be feeling, smile to the disappointment. Smile

to the experience of having emotions. Our emotions are messengers, and they signify something important in our world. Smiling to your emotions is a way to bring love and acceptance to what you are feeling. To honor and accept your feelings instead of suppressing them.

4. You are human. You have emotions. You have interpretations of what you experienced today. That is completely normal. Simply let it be as it is. Take a slow, deep breath as you affirm to yourself, "*I am human. I have emotions. I have interpreted what has happened today in a certain way, and I can just let that be. I don't need to make it mean anything about me. It has been my experience. It just is.*"

5. Take a slow, deep breath in and then sigh it out. Breathe in. Breathe out AH! In this process of affirming and accepting what is or what was, you can let go. Make that declaration right now. *I can let it go.* Breathe in. Breathe out. I am letting go right now in this moment. Imagine the heaviness or the disappointment releasing from your body and into the earth beneath your feet. Let it go. You are free.

6. Now connect with something you loved from your day—an experience, someone you encountered, something that happened. Just notice how you feel about that. And then smile to those feelings. Breathe into connection with whatever is present: possibly joy, fulfillment, happiness, excitement, peace. Let it permeate every cell of your body. Let it fill you up.

7. Breathe into that and say to yourself, "I *loved that experience. I love that person"* or *"I am so proud of myself. That was amazing."* Say whatever you need to say or communicate about your experience. Say that now. And then let it go. Imagine it being released from your body and into the earth beneath your feet. It is safe to let go. It is safe to relax. It is safe to surrender and to turn inward as you let go of today and as you get ready to have a peaceful night's sleep.

8. You can spend a few more minutes sitting in connection with yourself and your breath as you continue to let go and turn inward. Good night.

9

THE HIGHLY CRITICAL RELATIONSHIP

*Ultimately, we treat other people the way we treat
ourselves.*

For most of this book, we have looked at how feeling
not enough has impacted how we view ourselves. We
have identified how detrimental it can be to our self-
esteem and how it can negatively impact our ability
to create what we desire in our lives. In this chapter,
however, we will dive into how feeling *not enough* can
manifest in your relationships and can affect your
interactions with others.

When you have a highly developed, overactive
part of you that doesn't feel good enough, you may

find that you are extremely sensitive to others' criticism of you. Sometimes you may even be downright defensive and combative. You might be used to, and even okay with, being overly critical of yourself. But when someone criticizes you, it can quickly ruffle your feathers and put you on the defensive. Very simply, it is awakening the inadequacy you already feel. It's awakening the fear that you don't measure up, the fear that you don't have what it takes, the fear that you're not enough. This is one of the things that was driving the dysfunction in Jack's marriage.

JACK'S EXPLOSIVE TIRADES

Jack started working with me because he was extremely exhausted by how explosive the disagreements with his wife had become.

"Nothing is ever good enough for her," he shared. "In her eyes, I don't make enough money. She doesn't like how I parent our kids. She complains that I'm angry and defensive all the time. You know what? She's right. I am angry. I'm tired of feeling like a screw-up to her, like nothing I do is ever good enough."

Jack was at the end of his rope. He was stressed

out, anxious, and just flat-out miserable, at home, at work, and especially in his relationship with his wife. Not only was his marriage emotionally volatile, but worse, it was also awakening feelings of inadequacy from his childhood.

When we started diving into what Jack's upbringing was like, I wasn't surprised to hear that his dad was extremely critical of him, that he felt like nothing he ever did was good enough. It was one of the reasons Jack was defensive and why it was painful for him when his wife criticized him and said things that awakened those feelings of inadequacy from his childhood.

In our first coaching session, I invited Jack to connect to the little boy within him, the little boy who didn't get much attention or approval from his dad. I guided Jack to close his eyes and envision that little boy sitting in front of him.

"What does he look like, and how old is he?" I asked. Jack told me he was nine years old and looked a bit stoic—he seemed almost frozen in fear.

"Ask him to tell you how it felt not getting much affection, attention, or validation from his dad," I said.

Jack looked into the eyes of that little boy and listened. This is what he heard and what he shared with me.

He wasn't a very affectionate guy. I never got a hug when he left or when he came home. He showed up for my football games when he wasn't traveling for work, which wasn't very often. Sometimes I would get a pat on the back after a game. Sometimes I didn't. I remember one football game he attended. I was knocked down early in the game, and it took me a minute or two to get up off the field. After the game my dad said, "Son, you don't need to let people know you are hurt. You just keep playing." I can't even describe what that felt like. It crushed me because I knew I had let him down.

I invited Jack to stay connected to the shame he felt, to the feelings of inadequacy that little boy felt that night at the football game. I assured him that it would give him the insight and wisdom he needed to comfort that little boy who felt inadequate in his dad's eyes. By honoring what that little boy experienced, by allowing himself to see how harsh his dad's words were, Jack would be able to give himself permission to ease up on himself, to not beat himself up for that night any longer.

In addition to the inner work we did in his session, I gave Jack an assignment to comfort this little boy whenever his wife started to criticize him. To take a few minutes to disconnect from his wife and instead reconnect to that little boy, just like he did in his session. To silently or aloud express to the little boy that he is enough, that he is valuable, that he is worthy, just as he is. To understand that not only was he as the adult feeling the harshness of the criticism but also the little boy within him was being re-triggered in those moments. That's why it was so painful and why he became especially defensive and angry. By honoring himself and the pain this little boy had felt growing up, Jack would be able to comfort himself and stay grounded even when he was being criticized. He would be able to respond from a place of clarity and peace instead of being reactive and projecting his pain onto his relationship and his wife.

THE RELATIONSHIP MIRROR

Relationships can trigger our deepest wounds. If one of your relationships is awakening feelings of inadequacy, not feeling good enough, or feeling unworthy, know that although it can feel quite painful in the moment, this very relationship can be an immense source of growth and healing.

The key is to recognize what is happening in the

moment and honor what you need. Instead of focusing outward on your relationship and holding onto the hope that when it changes you will be OK, the work is to turn your attention inward and identify what limitation, fear, or inadequacy may be awakening from your past. Then instead of reacting to the emotional turmoil of the moment, you will be equipped to use it as a brilliant mirror into what's happening within you, gain the strength and insight to transcend any momentary discomfort or pain, and use it as an opportunity to heal, emerging stronger and more whole. Let's look at how you can use your relationship as a source of growth and healing with the exercises that follow.

BITE-SIZE EXERCISE

***

Identify the relationship in your life that is the most challenging for you right now. Make a commitment to use this relationship for the purpose of growth and healing by turning your attention toward how you are feeling and what it is awakening within you instead of focusing on what the other person is doing. Also, remind yourself over the next few days, as you interact with this person, that you are learning a new way of being in a relationship with yourself and others. And most importantly, it will become more harmonious over time.

Want more? Listen as I guide you through the exercise below on audio. Find the audio at www.dianealtomare.com/relationship-breakthrough-exercise

EXERCISE

Find a quiet place to do this visualization. Close your eyes, and as you take a slow, deep breath, notice the rise and fall of your chest and your abdomen. Take a few more

slow, deep breaths and begin. Write down what arises in your journal.

1. Imagine as you breathe into your heart that you can deeply connect with yourself and your breath. Just watch your breath, noticing that with your focus and attention on your breath, you can connect deeply to how you are currently feeling about yourself and your relationship.

2. Take a deep breath and allow yourself to connect to a conversation or situation in your relationship that you don't feel at peace with—something that feels unsettled or you don't feel good about.

3. Allow yourself to connect with the feelings that you are feeling about this relationship or situation. What does it feel like to be connected to this person in this way? Notice whatever feelings are present. Just breathe into those feelings and notice where in your body they live.

4. Take a deep breath and allow yourself to see how you are being triggered by this relationship or situation. How is this relationship causing you upset, dissatisfaction, or pain? Identify

specifically what is causing you to feel upset and write it down.

5. On your next breath, allow yourself to notice what this is triggering or bringing up for you from your past. Does this feel like something you have experienced before? Notice the ways this feels familiar to you. For example, she discounts how I feel just like my mom did. Or he isn't affectionate and doesn't listen to what I have to say. It feels like my relationship with my dad both growing up and now.

6. Take a deep breath and connect with what you most need to learn from this relationship. How is this relationship helping you to grow? Or what can you learn from this relationship? Listen as the answer to this question arises, "If this is the perfect experience, relationship, or challenge to help me grow, evolve, and become who I am meant to be, what am I supposed to be learning right now? How can this wisdom support me in creating my best year ever?"

7. Finally, ask yourself, "What action can I take this week to find peace within myself

regardless of the state of this relationship? What is one thing I can do to nurture myself and acknowledge how I am growing because of this very relationship?" Maybe you can practice disconnecting from your partner's feelings or identifying how learning this lesson from this relationship will help you develop into more of who you are meant to be.

8. Trust whatever answer comes to you. Just breathe into whatever this new realization is creating within you. Maybe you feel a little more peace or clarity. Jot down a few notes in your journal. Remember to put your action step in your calendar so you can complete the action that came from this exercise.

By observing what's happening instead of reacting, by looking at this very experience as a gift, our relationships can be a huge source of insight, healing, and growth.

Instead of battling it out with the other person or making them wrong, which sets up our relationship to have a winner and a loser, our work is to use it to go inward and heal a wounded part of ourselves.

As I shared in my first book, *Clarity*:

Most moments in your relationship that leave you feeling like there is no resolution, or leave you feeling frustrated, hopeless, or resigned, are gifts waiting to be uncovered. Those moments are a great indicator that there may be some way you are showing up in your relationship that mirrors or triggers an experience you had with a parent or sibling in childhood.

We can easily play out our childhood wounds in our relationships. Our partner, spouse, or in-law triggers us in some way, and we may trigger or affect that person as well. Then unconsciously or consciously, in order to "deal" with and deflect our feelings, we engage in a battle of pointing the finger away from ourselves and toward the other person. In that moment, we are simply showing up in our child self and the other person is showing up in their child self. We are replaying the unresolved experiences from our childhood and are acting out our wounds together. This inner-child-dueling-inner-child experience does not allow us to move beyond either the current issue or the past hurt. In this battle, we are simply placing our hurts and unresolved feelings onto the other person. We are making it the other person's fault that we feel the way we do or are being affected in a certain way. You may have experienced this in your relationship. It sounds something like this:

° "I hate the way you make me feel."
° "I can't deal with the way this relationship makes me feel."
° "Your actions hurt, you make me feel insecure, and when you stop doing that, I will be happy."

If we truly want to heal our own wounds, we must take back our projections and focus on how this relationship can help us grow. Once we do our own individual healing, we will be able to show up in the relationship in a new and more powerful way. We then won't be triggered as deeply by our relationship or will be able to recognize when we are negatively affected much more quickly.

The benefit of doing our own individual healing in our relationships is profound. The experience of the relationship becomes much more free, fun, and playful like it was at the beginning. In addition, when we aren't playing out "our unresolved pain"

from our childhood or bringing our past into our
relationships there is space to create something new.

BRAD AND CHLOE'S WAR ZONE

I started working with Brad and Chloe because their
marriage had become a war zone. There were many
different things contributing to the stress in their
relationship. However, the one that drove many of
their arguments was Brad's inability to deal with the
numerous ways he was triggered by his wife. He
found his wife to be overly demanding and harshly
critical and was starting to realize how many
unresolved wounds this was bringing up for him
from his childhood, mainly feelings of inadequacy.

Brad's dad was a classic narcissist. He shared that
he could never be wrong, always got the last word,
and was accusatory without giving Brad time to
explain his position or what had happened in any
given situation. Brad recalled always feeling like he
was less than his dad, not equally important, and
not worthy of the same love or respect that his dad
always demanded.

Fast-forward thirty years to Brad and Chloe's
relationship dynamic. What Brad craved most in his
relationship was respect and understanding because

he never received either as a child. However, instead of feeling like his wife respected him, Brad felt the opposite. He felt like he did as a child around his dad, like he was being belittled, reprimanded, and mostly, he felt inadequate. It was easy to see how Brad's marriage had become so volatile and chaotic. He was being triggered by his wife and he didn't yet have the tools to identify what wounds his relationship was awakening and how to comfort himself instead of projecting his anger and upset onto his relationship and onto his wife.

Brad's work was to first focus on acknowledging how the interactions in his marriage were awakening these wounds from his childhood and then to comfort the little boy within him who felt humiliated and insignificant. By doing this, he would be less vulnerable to the way Chloe criticized him and less apt to feel inadequate. He would also be able to consciously identify in any given moment how their dynamic was making him feel and show up as an adult instead of a wounded child.

I worked with each one of them in separate individual coaching sessions to address how each was being affected and triggered by the other. We then also worked together in couple's sessions. In our first few sessions, we talked about how each one of them was being impacted by the other and how essential it is to take care of yourself first. We simply can't be present in a relationship if we have a lot of inner turmoil going on. Worse, our unexpressed emotions, needs, and pain often create chaos in our relationship, because at some point, they get projected onto the other person.

We began one of their sessions with these three questions. Each gave them a helpful way to reflect on how they were feeling and what was truly going on.

> **Question One:** How do I feel about myself during our interactions?
>
> **Question Two:** How do I feel about my spouse during our interactions?
>
> **Question Three:** What feelings or past wounds are being awakened by our relationship dynamic? For example, feeling inadequate, unworthy, feeling like I'm not enough.

As Brad and Chloe shared what they were feeling, each one had the opportunity to truly listen to each other and find compassion for what was happening with their spouse because of their interactions and the chaos in their marriage.

BRAD'S FEELINGS

1. How do I feel about myself during our interactions? I feel small and like a child.
2. How do I feel about my spouse during our interactions? I can't stand being in the same room as her. I feel like she is the cause of all my pain.
3. What feelings or past wounds are being awakened by our relationship dynamic? I remember, as a kid, feeling so insignificant around my dad. I feel the same way around my wife.

CHLOE'S FEELINGS

1. How do I feel about myself during our interactions? His inability to see my point of view makes me so angry. It's always all about him and he can't handle any criticism at all. It makes it almost impossible to talk through things without him getting defensive and acting like a child.
2. How do I feel about my spouse during our interactions? I feel like I am the only adult in the room.

3. What feelings or past wounds are being awakened by our relationship dynamic? My dad was never around. All I want in a marriage is a strong man to show up, even when things are hard. I thought Brad was that man, but I guess he isn't.

Although it was painful for each one of them to be this raw, real, and honest about how they were feeling, it was essential to communicate their truth so they could begin to identify what was truly going on, what the deeper issues were. By listening to each other and expressing how they were feeling, they could finally, instead of pointing the finger at each other, start the journey to embracing what wounds were being awakened from their past. They both continued to do their own individual work to heal childhood wounds and work together in couple's sessions to have more compassion for each other's struggles. Slowly, week after week, their marriage became more harmonious. It was nothing short of fascinating to watch two people who continually at each other's throats, who were destroying each other, reconnecting and expressing their love and empathy for each other. This is what is available in even the most difficult relationships if we are willing to turn inward and identify how it is awakening a past wound and do the work to heal that hurt.

THE GIFT OF DIFFICULT RELATIONSHIPS

Relationships can be heart-wrenching. They can trigger our stuff, awaken old wounds, and even bring out the worst in us. On the flipside, they can be our greatest teacher and a source of immense love and joy.

Although it is sometimes extremely difficult, we must choose how we are going to show up in our relationships. Are we going to use the pain to grow, evolve, and experience more of what we need, more of what we desire in our relationship? Or are we going to avoid what is happening, let it fester for years, and resign ourselves to a place of hopelessness ensuring that one or both of us eventually choose not to be a part of the relationship anymore?

In the next chapter, we will dive deeply into the reservoir of stillness and peace that is available to you in any moment, an energy within you that will not only assist you in showing up gracefully and intentionally in your relationships but will also help you to feel more grounded and at peace in your life despite the challenges, setbacks, and difficult experiences.

10

GROUNDED IN MORE THAN ENOUGH

There is a current of stillness deep within you. A
well, a reservoir of resilience, joy, and peace. The
more you tap into it, the deeper connected you will
feel to yourself, your greatness, your soul.

Every morning at 5:30 a.m., you will find me
meditating. I have faithfully etched out this sacred
time to reconnect. I savor it every day. It's soulful. It
is everything to me.

It's a crucial time for me to connect to my soul,
to the intelligence of the universe, to God. To let
the happenings of life, the chaos in my mind melt
away. The result is nothing short of profound. Every

single time, I feel I am deepening a connection to myself and my truth. A significant amount of this book originated from this connection, from this stillness.

Depending on the morning, depending on my state of well-being, depending on what is going on in my life, I am met with a unique experience. Sometimes it is easy. Sometimes it's difficult. Sometimes my mind is racing; other times it is placid and still. Regardless, I sit in meditation for approximately forty-five minutes. I observe. I feel. I listen.

Many people have shared with me that they simply can't meditate. They can't get their mind to stop the constant madness. But that is the exact reason to sit in meditation every day. I know there can be a lot of chatter. I know it's not easy to sit still or to quiet your mind. However, when you allow the chatter to flow, when you sit in observation, eventually, over time, it dissipates. The chaos in your mind will melt away. You will be able to connect more deeply with the stillness within you. You will be able to access, within the space in between your thoughts, a reservoir of peace, the depth of your soul, the brilliance that you are.

The truth is you can only get to the stillness through the chatter. If you feel like the thoughts are running rampant, if you feel like it's tough to sit there, know that most of us have that experience, at least initially. Stay with it. Work through it. Give yourself the gift of letting that eventually melt away. So, you can experience the bliss, the immeasurable peace that is within you, that is always available to you, that is here to comfort you, to soothe your soul, to be utilized for remarkable things.

You have done so much work in this book shedding layers of societal conditioning and sifting through a lifetime of experiences, some of which have proven valuable throughout the years and others that have been limiting, that may still be limiting you right now. The deeper work lies in continuing to connect with yourself, to solidify your connection to your soul daily. This is exactly what we will be deeply diving into throughout this chapter.

But before you explore this deeper connection to yourself, including the daily practice you may want to begin to implement, let's take a moment to look back at what you have already accomplished and how you may want to use these pages moving forward.

FIRST, A LOOK BACK

The purpose of reviewing the work you have done thus far is twofold. First, to take time to acknowledge yourself for what you have accomplished. And second, to give you a place to earmark and revisit whenever you need to find something useful to transcend or embrace whatever you're experiencing. Let's look at what you have explored, learned, and gained from each chapter.

CHAPTER ONE

In chapter 1, you began to explore the part of you that doesn't feel good enough and how it may be keeping you from creating what you want or stopping you from experiencing the richness life has to offer.

If you find yourself being especially critical, dive into chapter 1, especially the exercise at the end of the chapter. You will gain the insight you need to recognize the impact your harsh, critical inner voice is having on your self-esteem, soften your inner dialogue, become more kind, encouraging, and loving to yourself, and create more of what you desire.

CHAPTER TWO

In chapter 2, we looked at where your not-good-enough self originated from. The more intimately connected you become to the reason you don't feel good enough, worthy enough, smart enough, talented enough or whatever not enough you continually judge yourself for, the easier it will be to have compassion for yourself and begin to shift how you're talking to yourself, which voice you're listening to, and the way you're treating yourself every day.

If you find the negative voice in your head taking over and controlling your day, revisit chapter 2 and do the exercise in the middle of the chapter. It will remind you that there is a reason you are the way you are and will give you the insight you may need to have more compassion for yourself.

CHAPTER THREE

In chapter 3, we explored one of the ways to begin to change the way you are talking to yourself. We also acknowledged an important truth: the part of you that doesn't feel good enough is simply a part of you, it is not who you are in totality. At the same time, you have the power to connect with the empowering, life-affirming part of you that feels more than enough, that is powerful, wise, and knows that you are brilliant enough, talented enough, courageous enough, and powerful enough to fulfill your life's purpose and live your best life.

If you need a confidence boost, dive into chapter 3, especially the "Talk to Yourself with Love" exercise.

CHAPTER FOUR

In chapter 4, we identified how everything you explored up to that point could support you in having more of what you want in your life. You continued to solidify your connection with your more-than-enough self and may have felt it awakening powerful, inspiring energy.

If you feel that you are sabotaging yourself or your dreams, dive into chapter 4 and give your not-good-enough self a voice. By envisioning this part of you as an ally, and gaining the wisdom it has to offer, you will be equipped to move powerfully forward in alignment with your goals instead of letting it take ᴺᵈ take you off course.

CHAPTER FIVE

In chapter 5, I asked you to reflect on this illuminating question, "If my heart's desires are aligned with my highest self, are arising from the depth of my soul, and are part of my life's purpose, why wouldn't I be able to create what I desire?"

It's an empowering question that deserves great thought. Through your reflection and your work in chapter 5, the goal is to get to the place where you are not only pondering this truth but also believing it in the depth of your soul, and most importantly, acting on it wholeheartedly in your life. If you need inspiration or fuel to create more of what you desire, if you need the energy that comes from embracing how unique, amazing, talented, and truly magnificent you are, dive into chapter 5.

CHAPTER SIX

In chapter 6, we deeply explored self-doubt, which is one of the biggest obstacles you may encounter on the journey to staying connected to your more than enough self and creating your best life. Self-doubt can be a dream killer and can be extremely debilitating on the journey to creating what we desire.

Most of us know what it feels like to flip-flop back and forth through being powerfully connected to our truth and greatness one minute, forging ahead wholeheartedly in our life, and the next moment allowing self-doubt and fear to instantaneously turn our motivation and inspiration upside down, rapidly careening us back to the shores of safety and familiarity. If you find that self-doubt is keeping you stuck or making you feel bad about yourself, use the "Infuse Energy" exercise in chapter 6 to reconnect to who you truly are and what is going well in your life.

CHAPTER SEVEN

In chapter 7, we talked about how detrimental comparing ourselves to others can be. It can negatively impact our mental and emotional well-being if we use it to make ourselves feel bad. And even more damaging, if it stops us from focusing on, tending to, or creating what we want in our own lives. It can render us powerless at times.

Think about how extremely unfair it is to ⁀ᵃ someone's amazing, picture-perfect ficult day you are having or a struggle And yet, sometimes, we do it anyway.

If you find yourself resigned to a life that doesn't inspire you, and are continually comparing yourself to others, chapter 7 will help you to stop beating yourself up in this way, and instead use it as a gift to catapult you back into action, shining your light brighter and creating more of what you desire in your life.

CHAPTER EIGHT

In chapter 8, we explored how feeling not good enough can create stress, overwhelm, and an imbalance in our lives. This isn't altogether negative, as there is a healthy drive within each of us that compels us to strive, create, evolve, and move beyond our current circumstances.

However, for some of us, especially those who have an overdeveloped, highly dysfunctional not-good-enough self, this force can become all consuming, taking over, kicking us into overdrive, and pushing us until we are exhausted and begging for mercy. If you find that you are never satisfied, that nothing is ever enough, that you are constantly moving from one task to the next, dive into chapter 8 to regain your footing when you feel overwhelmed, anxious, or out of balance.

CHAPTER NINE

In chapter 9, we explored how not feeling good enough manifests in your relationships and your interactions with others.

If you are in a relationship that is exhausting or continually challenging because either you or the other person is projecting their feelings of inadequacy onto the relationship, dive into chapter nine to connect to what is truly happening so you can respond from a place of clarity and peace instead of being reactive.

NOW, A LOOK FORWARD

I hope as you reviewed the work you did in each chapter, you acknowledged yourself for the remarkable journey you have taken—a glorious journey of reconnecting to your truth, your greatness, your soul. Anytime you need to, you can use these past few pages as a reference to determine ᵗ·ᵗʰ chapter you may want to revisit.

ᵗɔok forward to what's possible,
ᵗ you may want to include in your
ɪur sacred time to reflect and to deepen

your connection to yourself, your truth, your greatness, your soul.

CREATING YOUR DAILY PRACTICE

I have coached clients from all walks of life, from many different religions, and many different beliefs. Many of my clients have incorporated some type of sacred time to connect with themselves every day. Each person's sacred time is unique. Ultimately, it will represent you, your beliefs, your values, what makes you feel most connected to yourself and your soul. It may be religious. It may be spiritual. It may not. What matters most is that it feels good to you. That it fills you up, that it deepens your connection to yourself, that it is rejuvenating to you and your soul, that it reconnects you, replenishes you, and is something you are willing to do consistently.

Below are some of the ways my clients have created this daily structure for themselves. You can pick one of these to start with or create a ritual of your own.

SACRED RITUALS

Sacred Ritual Idea One:

First thing every morning, Sarah opens her favorite sacred book. From a place of stillness in her soul and silence in her home, she spends the first fifteen minutes of her day reading and getting inspired. She finishes her routine with a prayer that fills her with both courage and compassion for herself and others.

Sacred Ritual Idea Two:

After my client, Rebecca, gets her morning cup of coffee, she sits in a cozy chair by her fireplace and tunes into God with a prayer. She spends at least ten minutes sipping her coffee and praying by the fire before she starts her day. Getting grounded and tuned in starts her day off on a solid footing, deeply connected to herself and to God.

Sacred Ritual Idea Three:

Every night, my client, Allison, gets in her cozy PJs, jumps into bed, and begins her nighttime ritual which consists of a fifteen-minute meditation of ʰing and daily reflection. As she focuses she notices how she feels about her ɪt she feels good about and what she wants to improve upon. She finishes her ritual by writing down what she is grateful for in her journal.

Sacred Ritual Idea Four:

At three o'clock in the afternoon, my client, AJ, closes the door to her office, turns off her phone, and sits in quiet reflection for ten minutes. She finds that this brief time of silence and solitude gives her energy and helps ground her in strength and peace as she finishes her workday. Although her workday is hectic, she diligently guards this time for herself.

Sacred Ritual Idea Five:

Before my client, John, begins his drive home from work, he sits in the parking garage and takes seven minutes to reflect, to observe how he is doing, to connect with how he is feeling after his long workday. He uses deep breathing to intentionally release anything that is still on his mind, anything unresolved that may need to be addressed the next day. He then smiles in anticipation of his drive home as he prepares to listen to his favorite jazz music so that he can arrive home relaxed and ready to spend time with his wife and kids.

Sacred Ritual Idea Six:

As I shared at the onset of this chapter, my daily

ritual starts out at 5:30 a.m. sitting by the fire in my living room with a cup of my favorite hot tea. I begin with deep breathing exercises, balancing both the observation of my thoughts as they arise and silently reciting this mantra at different points throughout:

"Attuning to the harmony of my body, my breath, my divine spirit, the intelligence of the universe, and God. Letting all else melt away."

Another mantra I love and use often:

"Attuning to the deep stillness within me, the resilience, the joy, the peace. Letting all else melt away."

My intention is to observe, be present, surrender, and deeply connect. I always leave feeling calmer, stronger, and refreshed.

Now it's your turn to create your ritual. A sacred time to connect, a meditation practice, a prayer practice, a morning ritual, a nighttime ritual, or whatever practice will reconnect you to yourself and feed your soul.

EXERCISE

YOUR TURN: CREATE YOUR SACRED RITUAL

In this exercise, you will have the chance to explore a daily ritual or structure that will ground you, energize you, and give you inspiration every day. By identifying what you can do to fill yourself up and deepen your connection to yourself, you will have a ritual that is rejuvenating to you and your soul. Find a quiet place to do this visualization and begin.

1. Close your eyes and take a slow, deep breath and follow that breath inside, noticing the rise and fall of your chest and your abdomen.
2. As you take another deep breath, identify when you feel most grounded, centered, peaceful, and deeply connected to yourself, such as during deep breathing exercises, meditation, yoga, prayer, reading sacred text, walking, journaling, and so on.

Take a moment to jot down a few notes about what would support you in feeling more calm, connected, and grounded.

3. Take a deep breath and connect with your heart and a sacred ritual that will support you in having more of what you need in your life right now. Do you need a meditation practice or a prayer practice? Does your sacred time to connect feel more suited for a morning ritual or a nighttime ritual?

4. Continue to take a few slow, deep breaths, noticing the rise and the fall of your chest and abdomen, with each inhale and each exhale, as you explore how long you will give your sacred ritual each day. Just think about the next seven days for now. How much time are you willing to devote to your sacred ritual each day?

5. On your next breath, breathe into your heart and allow yourself to connect with what would be available to you by committing to this daily ritual. Would you feel more grounded, more peace, harmony, joy, or inspiration? Envision yourself feeling more connected to your truth, more centered. As you do, jot down some

notes about what it will feel like to create your life from this inspired place.

6. Put your hand on your heart and breathe this into every cell of your being, allowing it to fill you up with energy, joy, peace, fulfillment, inspiration, creativity, and anything else that may be arising for you.

7. Breathe again into your heart and make a commitment to put this new ritual you have created for yourself into practice every day.

Your work is to begin your sacred ritual. For the next seven days, as you begin and as you complete your daily ritual, notice how you feel about your sacred time and then make any adjustments you see fit. Maybe you need to increase the time you devote to this ritual as you have noticed that it takes a while for your thoughts to clear out, to dissipate. Maybe it needs to be shorter or earlier in the morning to fit into your daily routine. Maybe you need to explore different breathing exercises to keep you engaged. Whatever changes may be needed, let this be a working exploration until you find a daily ritual that feels right to you, remembering that the sole purpose of creating this daily structure is to deepen your connection to yourself, your greatness, your soul.

BITE-SIZE EXERCISE

***

Spend a few minutes right now connecting to the silence and stillness within you. Take some slow, deep breaths, and give yourself permission to let everything go. Breathe in. Breathe out. Breathe in. Breathe out. Simply follow your breath inside and observe whatever is present. Your thoughts may run rampant, your emotions may be swirling. Whatever you observe or feel is perfect. Spend four minutes in this space before you wholeheartedly dive into the last few paragraphs of this book. Let these words encode your consciousness and fill your divine soul with everything you need.

THE SOLE PURPOSE

The sole aim of everything we have done in this book is to give you a deeper understanding of how to stop the critical, judgmental internal war from raging on. To bring you into connection with your spirit, your soul, to the only real peace that exists. To solidify your union with the *you* that doesn't define a momentary experience as *not enough* and knows that the part of you that doesn't feel *good enough* is simply a part of your human experience, it is not who you are. To reconnect you to the *you* that knows that whatever pain or challenge you are experiencing is only a sliver of the human condition and can't define the magnificence that you are. The magnificence you have always been. That you will always be.

The entire journey of life is about returning to this truth.

I hope you have felt the power of your soul, of your significance, of your magnificence. Or just seen glimpses of it at various times throughout this book. Whatever your experience has been, know that there is a current of stillness deep within you. A well, a reservoir of peace, resilience, and joy that knows only love. A place where you are whole, you are enough, and that nothing in this human experience can ever permanently sever that.

It is unbreakable, unshakable, unaffected by the storms of the world or the rocky, turbulent nature of the human condition. Once you feel that truth, it is one that will always be available to you regardless of what may be going on in your life or the world around you. Let that fill you with peace, with love, with whatever you may need in any moment.

This is the journey, this is the work, this is the freedom available to you—always.

I hope you will continue to use this book as a guide into the deep reservoir of love and peace within you. To know you have the power to tap into it at any time. To become one with it. To emanate the greatness that you are, that you have always been, that you will always be. Love, Diane

WHAT'S NEXT

Every week, I share wisdom and inspiration with my community of thousands of people striving to make each day of their lives matter, committed to making a difference, and living an inspired life. You can get this wisdom and inspiration delivered your inbox by signing up here:

DianeAltomare.com/email

ACKNOWLEDGMENTS

From the deepest place in my heart, I thank everyone who has supported me and contributed to this book. I love the written word. I love being a part of transforming people's lives. I love transforming my own. Words could never express the immense gratitude I feel for being the author of this book, the messenger of this wisdom. It is a bittersweet feeling now that it is complete as I have thoroughly enjoyed every moment of writing it. This book has been in the works for the past twenty years, through both the remarkable healing journey of my life and with every client I have had the honor of coaching, guiding, and supporting in their journey of growth and healing.

To Arielle Ford and Brian Hilliard, thank you from the bottom of my heart for your dear friendship. For your support of my writing and my work. For your generosity and your huge contribution to bringing my books into the world.

I cherish you and your love, support, and divine wisdom more than you can ever know.

To Debbie Ford, with tears of gratitude, I still cry when I think about how grateful I am to have known you in this lifetime when I reflect on the impact you have had on my life. You taught me how to love myself, and that is the biggest gift one can give another human being. Although you are not physically here on this earthly plane, our connection grows deeper year after year, and so does my gratitude for you, your work, and your legacy.

To Susan Harrow, your contribution to continuing to bring my work into the world has been beyond profound. Thank you for helping me be intentional with my communication and message.

To the amazing staff at Waterside Productions for your expertise and immense dedication to this book.

To my agent, Bill Gladstone, for your belief in my work all these years.

To Lisa Breckenridge, for your unwavering support and love, and for our collaboration of the Embracing Your Greatness series. I loved working on that project with you.

To Denise Dador, I am so grateful we had the opportunity to work together on the forgiveness segment. I remember the moment when I first saw that powerful three-minute clip all put together. I have the utmost respect for you, your expertise, and how brilliantly you can craft a story and bring it to life on screen.

To every one of my clients, it has been one of the greatest joys of my life to be an integrative coach. You truly made the wisdom in this book possible as you shared your life, your struggles, and your biggest dreams with me over the past twenty years.

To Jeffrey Malone, Clifford Edwards, Donna Lipman, and Anne Browning for your love, support, and immense contribution to my growth.

To Julie Stroud and Kelley Kosow for continuing the work of the Ford Institute of Integrative Coaching and keeping us all connected. I am forever grateful to you both.

To Mary Lou Yoch, for being such a dear friend over the years. Even though we live on opposite coasts, it comforts me to know you are just a phone call away.

To Pat Worns, for your witty humor, moxie, and strength. I adore you and our illuminating conversations. You have touched my life in so many ways.

To my Aunt Margaret, for the way you always made me feel loved, accepted, and at home. I miss you.

To Steve Newman, for saying, "Do what you

love... nothing else matters." You gave me the most poignant piece of advice I ever received. It truly directed my journey and my life and led me to find the happiness and fulfillment I was always striving for.

To my husband and best friend, Christopher, for your never-ending support and love year after year through the pursuit of my biggest dreams. It takes immense time and dedication to write a book, and you have always supported my work, my quirkiness, and everything it takes to keep me thriving, which we both know is a lot. And to Alexandra—you will always be my sweet baby girl even though you are all grown up. Words could never express how proud I am of who you have become and how grateful I am to forever be your mom. I am the luckiest girl to be both of yours. You two are my heart.

1. Debbie Ford, Your Holiness: Discover the Light Within (HarperOne, 2018), p. 104.

ABOUT THE AUTHOR

DIANE ALTOMARE is a Master Certified Integrative Life Coach to thousands of people worldwide. She has been featured on NBC, ABC7 News, more than thirty local and nationally syndicated radio shows, including CBS Radio and NPR, and has contributed to many publications including mindbodygreen, AARP, and the Chicago Tribune.

For the past twenty years as a beloved motivational speaker and workshop leader, she has helped thousands of people transform from a limiting past to an inspiring future. Known as "the coach with the authentic, gentle, and laser-focused approach," she has a gift for nailing the deep truth behind any situation.

Diane received her certification and extensive training as a Master Level Certified Coach from the Ford Institute of Integrative Coaching, founded by Debbie Ford, and holds a Bachelor of Arts in Interdisciplinary Studies from the University of South Carolina.

She is also the author of *Clarity: 10 Proven Strategies to Transform Your Life*, which jumped to #1 New Release on Amazon in Emotional Self-Help.

Made in the USA
Columbia, SC
02 May 2024

34849156R00113